A·SENSE OF THE PAST

A SENSE OF THE PAST

GRAEME GARDEN

with Graham Nown

WARD LOCK LIMITED · LONDON

© Graham Nown 1985

First published in Great Britain in 1985
by Ward Lock Limited, 82 Gower Street,
London WC1E 6EQ, an Egmont Company.

Text set in Bembo
by DP Press, Sevenoaks, Kent.

Printed and bound in Great Britain
by Hazell Watson & Viney Ltd, Aylesbury.

British Library Cataloguing in Publication Data

Garden, Graeme
  A sense of the past.
  1. England——History, Local   2. England——
  Historiography
  I. Title   II. Nown, Graham
  942   DA1

  ISBN 0-7063-6345-0

A Sense of the Past is a ⅄ Yorkshire Television production

Producer: David Wilson
Associate Producer: Michael Harris
Director: Ann Ayoub
Education Officer: Michael Scarborough

CONTENTS

ACKNOWLEDGEMENTS

Grateful thanks for the efforts, advice and co-operation of Gordon Borthwick, CAMRA, Fred and Chris Cooke, Dr James Stevens Curl, Christopher Driver, Patrick Green, Tony Howarth, Clyde Jeavons, David Jenkinson, Alan King, Audrey Linkman, Julian Litten, Robert Opie, Chris Palmer, Jean Pateman, Ken Powell, George Redmans, Arthur Saul, David Sekers, John Spencer, Gavin Stamp, Rodney Taylor, Dr John Whiteleg.

. . . And especially to David Wilson, Ann Ayoub and Mike Harris without whom this book would not have been possible.

We would also like to thank the following for permission to reproduce illustrations in the book: Hoover, House of Fraser, Kodak Museum, Liverpool City Council, Manchester Studies, National Film Archive, National Trust for Scotland, Nicholson's Freehouses, Portsmouth City Museum, Bob Preedy, Robert Opie Collection, Yorkshire Television Stills Department, David Wilson.

A Sense of the Past is a Yorkshire Television production.

INTRODUCTION

Every day we all experience a sense of the past. We see it everywhere – a Victorian Town Hall, a War Memorial, a Vintage car, a silent movie on television, a Roman road, a factory chimney, a Punk hair-style. We are surrounded by indications of the way we used to live in years gone by. Most of the time we hardly notice them, and yet they can help us to learn about, and understand, the development of our society. Our heritage is rich, but will future generations have so many clues to their past around them?

Too often, when we were preparing this book and television series, our researchers would arrive to see some piece of architecture, or engineering, or landscape, only to be told 'Oh, if only you'd been here last week . . .' Or last month, or last year, before the architecture was demolished, the engineering modernized, the landscape developed. We simply weren't there in time.

None of us can afford to take these fascinating clues to the past for granted. Remember, we only miss them when they're gone.

Graeme Garden

1

IT'S THE FOURTH LEG WHICH CAUSES THE WOBBLE

It's a refreshing thought that we can drink history. The Great British Pint goes back a long time, and our ale-houses, too, have a rich tradition which we can all help to preserve every time we go into a pub. Ale has been drunk in Britain since Roman times – perhaps even earlier – and over the centuries it has changed and evolved. For example, in the nineteenth century, with the addition of hops during the brewing process, beer was produced which replaced ale. The places in which we drink have also changed.

The pub, as we know it today, is a comparatively recent institution, founded and encouraged to curb a national epidemic of gin drinking. The image of Old England we see on biscuit tins and Christmas cards was quite a different story. Happy rustics, quaffing mugs of ale on the village green outside a thatched inn, portray the rural life of coaching houses and the traveller's rest. Ancient inns were built and run to provide food and rest for the traveller and, as such, were not really pubs as we know them. They guaranteed warmth and good company and, on high days and holidays, a place of merriment, music and intoxication. There are, of course, many

The Victorian pub in all its cut-glass glory: The Argyll, in London's West End.

'The Traps' at the Argyll – a tiny Victorian front bar from the days when women customers drank separately from men.

accounts of the stench, fleas in the bedrooms and a general lack of sanitation, but they were also the centre of social life and enjoyment after a hard day's work.

While conditions in the country were poor, in the cities they were appalling. As overcrowding, poverty and despair grew, drinking began to take an evil turn. In an urge to forget their circumstances, adults and children drank cheap gin of terrible quality in increasing amounts. It was the drink of working people, and 'Drunk for a penny – dead drunk for tuppence' became the motto of thousands. Violence, alcoholism and child abuse became commonplace – the nightmare summed up by Hogarth's famous engraving Gin Street.

In 1830 the Duke of Wellington, who was Prime Minister became deeply concerned about the effect that gin drinking was having on the population. His solution was the Beer Houses Act which enabled any householder to hand over £2 and obtain a licence to sell beer at home. Beer houses were not allowed to sell spirits, and gin was heavily taxed. Gradually gin became an up-market drink, and beer the beverage of the masses. The result was that the number of beer houses in cities doubled within five years, and the consumption of 'mother's ruin' slumped dramatically. The public house was born. Ordinary homes throughout the country were adapted and opened their doors.

Beer was served from jugs in the kitchen, which became known as the tap room. As business boomed the better-off guests were served in the parlour, while

14

poorer customers huddled round the tap-room fire. As other private rooms were opened up into bars, snugs or smoke rooms, the familiar pattern of the public house evolved.

Victorian cities expanded and the splendid, purpose-built pubs we know today began to make their appearance. But what about the beer? By about 1880 even the weakest beer brewed in the hundreds of back street breweries was more potent than the strongest beer brewed today. People, young and old, drank it before they went to work and drank it when they came home – presumably their constitutions were more robust than ours.

In the nineteenth century there were no restrictions on children going into public houses and ordering themselves a pint. Many adults drank beer for remedial purposes. Steelworkers in Sheffield, and glassworkers from St Helens to Fulham downed it to replace the sweat they lost at the furnaces. Hospitals served beer daily to their patients, and generally it was more socially acceptable than today.

But as its popularity spread there was one body of people who saw drinking as a social evil. The temperance movement believed that even a mug of beer at the end of the day was a step on the road to moral decay and damnation. They toured the country with tableaux and lantern slides preaching the perils of the demon drink.

These would have included a lantern-slide soap opera of the day called *Buy Your Own Cherries*, a hand-coloured homily on the dangers of beer. The moral tone is high and dramatic: a working man leans on the bar of his local, spending his wages on drink and bad company. At home, his wife despairs of the future and the children wonder when the next meal will be.

One day he argues with the barmaid about a bowl of cherries on the bar. 'Get your own cherries!' she tells him. Next pay day he wonders – shall he buy the drink, or the cherries for his family? The cherries win, and the family has food again. The husband returns to the bosom of his family and the cupboard is no longer bare. In the final lantern slide, the predictable moral flickers onto the screen: 'If you would have a home sweet home, you must buy your own.'

At the height of the temperance movement there were many institutions upholding the belief that good health and abstention go hand in hand. These included

ABOVE: *Fitzpatrick's temperance bar – last bastion of the might of the temperance movement.*

BELOW: *A Glasgow tea room, designed for the temperance movement by Scotland's greatest exponent of Art Nouveau, Charles Rennie Mackintosh.*

coffee houses, refreshment rooms, hotels, ballrooms, building societies and a most common sight at this time – the temperance bar. The last remaining temperance bar in Britain still stands, on a windy corner in Rawtenstall, Lancashire. Fitzpatrick's has a bar like any other local, but the favourite brew is sarsaparilla. Alternatively you can order blood beer with raisins, orange and lemon and cream soda. It is still a popular place with locals, who regard it as a bar for all the family. You can buy packets of home brew sarsaparilla and herbal remedies for every

eventuality whicn include nerve pills, strength tablets, and anaemic capsules. The belief endures that good health and abstention go hand in hand. You can build up your heart, gain strength and clarity and purify your blood or liver – reinforcing the herbal regimen with health-giving sarsaparilla.

Another approach to winning people away from the demon drink started in Scotland, and has all but disappeared in its original form – the tea room. The idea was to attract the drinking public with splendid fittings and a convivial atmosphere. They became

so popular that it was said that Glasgow was 'the very Tokyo for tea rooms.'

Kate Cranston, suffragette and daughter of a wealthy family, was the remarkable woman who took on Scotland's drinkers – and there were no half-measures. She employed the top architects of the day, like Charles Rennie Mackintosh, to design her tea rooms. They were the very model of respectability and gentility, in every way the opposite of Sauchiehall Street's wild whisky bars. Today they are shops and offices but, here and there, the first blossoming of

OPPOSITE LEFT: *Pubs in mining areas were popular meeting places for customers and their dogs. Whippet racing is still a favourite pastime after closing time on Sunday afternoons.*

TOP RIGHT: *Pubs have always been an important part of the community – these regulars from the Gardener's Arms, Bolton, pose for a picture before their annual picnic.*

BOTTOM RIGHT: *Waiting for business in a pub which dispensed cream toffees along with the drinks – one of the forerunners of the off-licence.*

the light, elegant style of Scottish Art Nouveau can still be seen.

In their heyday, many had special rooms where you could read, or do business. Tea rooms long outlived the temperance movement, falling into decline in the fickle, faster-moving 1950s. They were, however, effective enough to worry the brewers, who fought back with a vengeance. The first thing they did was to improve the image of their bars with tasteful and high-class decor. There is a well-preserved example in Sloane's Restaurant in Glasgow, a far cry from the whisky bar. The restaurant itself was a red herring to lend respectability to drinking in the bar downstairs.

Although slightly modernized, it stands as an example of Victorian interior decoration at its most exuberant – a palace of carved wood, engraved glass and polished brass. Attention to detail is beautiful, but practical: a skilfully designed island bar allows faster service for more people. Where you can now

hear the chattering of a fruit machine, and the smell of pub grub, it is not difficult to imagine yourself back in more elegant times.

Some way away the twentieth-century façade of Glasgow's Old Toll Bar hides a pub which is almost exactly as it was. Grimy working men were tempted and flattered by the grand and elegant decor. They savoured their pint in the kind of environment we would now associate with an antique shop –

Many old pubs retain their traditional three-legged cast-iron tables. Unlike the four-legged ones we use today, they solve the problem of uneven floors. Stand a three-legged table on a rough stone surface, and it remains perfectly stable – it's the fourth leg which causes the wobble. The mind behind the brilliantly simple idea is thought to be that of bridge-builder Isambard Kingdom Brunel.

Cut glass, polished wood and velvet – the Victorian pub lovingly preserved.

The pleasure of a well-kept pint in a traditional pub preserved in all its splendour.

Some of the early breweries, like one at Stamford, have been preserved for visitors. Thousands of them sprang up in nineteenth-century Britain to meet the great beer boom.

magnificent mirrors, gleaming mahogany and the dappled hues of stained glass. The atmosphere is still quiet and unhurried, reflecting the beauty of the surroundings.

Glasgow bars are open twelve hours a day, which seems quite liberal compared with the nine hours pubs are open in England. But, like the pub itself, licensing hours are quite a new development.

The earliest drinking restrictions were made in the nineteenth century, when London pubs were prohibited from opening from midnight on Saturday until lunchtime Sunday. Modern licensing hours date from the Great War when Lloyd George, who was Minister of Munitions and himself a tee-totaller, imposed restrictions because he was worried about

workers keeping up the war effort. They have stayed ever since. The first real licensing Act, in the 1920s, set the standards with which we comply today.

CAMRA, which in the last ten years has brought the plight of British beer to the public eye and swayed the major brewers, is now turning its attention to licensing hours. But perhaps a more important issue is the danger facing the pub itself. Preservation groups keep a watchful eye on planning applications, and generally monitor the movements of the big breweries. If a village pub is to be sold off on purely economic grounds, with no consideration for the local community, petitions are drawn up and protests organized. A typical example was the Garden Gate, a Victorian Leeds pub, earmarked for demolition by planners in the 1960s. It was saved and today does thriving business in the middle of a modern housing development.

Most of our cities are Victorian, with lots of Victorian pubs – if you can still manage to spot them behind the Formica, the neon, the keg beer and the Space Invaders. But if you look carefully the clues are still there.

The Irreplaceable Pub

Pubs are an essential part of the community. You can't buy a pint in a post office, but you can buy a stamp in a pub. There is even an inn in Shropshire where you can vote – it doubles as a polling station at election time. In the Yorkshire Dales you can cash a cheque – a local pub is turned into a bank one morning a week. In Northumberland there is a pub where church services are held every Sunday morning.

Real British beer, which has a long history, had its most dangerous hour in the 1960s when it was nearly replaced with identifizz. But now we can once again conjure up the image of the friendly landlord, muscles bulging as he pulls a pint from the great wooden casks. . . . Even of him stirring steaming, richly smelling vats as he prepares more of his potent brew. For an increasing number of pubs are now brewing on the premises, just as they did before the breweries took over.

Sheffield's Frog and Parrot is a fine example, expanded by a brewery into a vision of the future. Music is made by an upright piano in an attempt to recapture not only the beer, but the atmosphere of the traditional British pub. The landlord brews his beer as the customers need it, to suit local taste. Finally, after the dark days of the 1960s and 1970s, the public and the brewers are recognizing the importance of the Great British Pub.

CAMRA Shy

The biggest, and most dramatic change happened in the 1960s when the big brewers tried to standardize the Great British Pint with gassy keg ales. The reaction was the birth of CAMRA, the most successful consumer movement Europe has ever seen.

In 1971 it took on the big six brewers who were buying up a number of small breweries all over Britain. Ultimately, says CAMRA, there would have been one beer throughout the country. The same pint would have been on sale from Glasgow to Greenwich, without any difference in taste.

The small group of enthusiasts demanded properly brewed beer, drawn out of the pumps by muscle power, not forced from a tap by pressurized carbon dioxide. Membership increased to 40,000, and the breweries once again started brewing some real ales.

Although the emphasis is still on keg beers, real ale is back, and the hand pump is making a reappearance on Britain's bar tops.

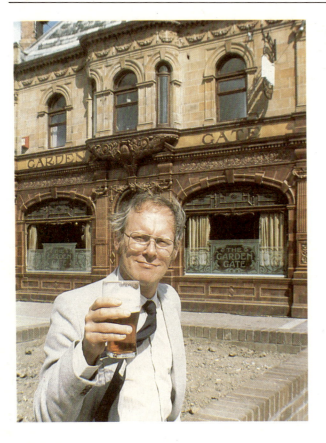

Some Victorian pubs have been successfully saved from demolition and incorporated into modern housing areas.

FIND OUT FOR YOURSELF

Campaign for Real Ale (CAMRA)
34 Alma Road
St Albans AL1 3BW
Hertfordshire.
CAMRA welcomes hearing from anyone who cares, not only about the fabric of the place in which they drink, but also the quality and taste of real traditional beer.

The Bass Museum
Horninglow Street
Burton upon Trent DE14 1JZ
Staffordshire.
Britain's most important open brewing museum, with a main exhibition which traces the development of brewing in Burton from earliest times. It has a Cooper's shop, reconstructed brewer's office, shire horses, steam dray – and a licensed lunchtime bar.

Stamford Brewery Museum
All Saints Street
Stamford PE9 2PA
Lincolnshire.
See a complete Victorian brewery, with a cooper, wheelwright and saddler at work. Beautiful shire horses too.

2

THE GREAT UNWASHED

Alongside the great strides of nineteenth-century progress made by industry, railways, ships and buildings, trotted a modest little achievement. On a rather chilly February morning in 1852, the Society of Arts unveiled a new masterpiece in Fleet Street – the first public lavatory. It was for the convenience of gentlemen; a euphemistically-titled 'waiting room for ladies' opened its doors off the Strand, just nine days later. The idea had been tentatively introduced twelve months earlier at the Crystal Palace Great Exhibition, but not without some controversy. Despite the robust personal habits of the masses in London's thoroughfares, the better-off were not used to 'doing it' in public.

Sir Henry Cole, originator of the Christmas card, and a distinguished sponsor of the Great Exhibition, was an enthusiastic promoter of the public water closet. He persuaded Sir Samuel Morton Peto, builder of Nelson's Column, to embark on the Fleet Street enterprise in the highest public interest. They were no doubt further spurred by the promise of pleasing returns – the Great Exhibition lavatory had made a handsome profit of £1,500 in just six months.

But it was not to be. The pioneer venture had to be abandoned due to lack of patronage. The 'waiting room' in Bedford Street, off the Strand, was frequented on average by only one lady per day. Gentlemen were hardly more adventurous. Advertisements in *The Times*, and leaflets distributed in the streets explaining its function, failed to lure them into new experience. By the end of the month fewer than sixty customers had cautiously relieved themselves in Fleet Street.

For the next three years the population of the metropolis presumably made their own arrangements until, in 1855, the City of London proudly opened an underground public lavatory, opposite the Royal Exchange. Even at a penny a visit it was clearly a bargain for hard-pressed businessmen, and its popularity grew. Glorious examples in gleaming brass and tiles, with exuberant carvings and foliate columns, began to spring up all over Britain. Vaulted subterranean palaces echoed to the music of flushing water. By the late nineteenth century the sanitary industry was booming, led by familiar names, such as Twyfords and Shanks. It would have happened

Marble and memorable ceramics in the Victorian lavatory of a Yorkshire town hall.

23

earlier, if Victorian mechanical engineering had not been hampered by lack of a proper water supply.

The first real breakthrough came in 1859 when 1000 miles of sewers, designed by Bazelgette, were constructed to drain London. The huge undertaking took six years to complete, but most importantly, an example had been set. The great industrial cities followed suit, and built their own effluent systems in grand style. Up until then death and disease had flourished in our rivers as the effluents from our growing cities were dumped untreated into them. The twin killers of cholera and typhoid spread through the population, claiming thousands of victims. Conditions were appalling in the cramped slums where sanitation, often little more than an earth pit, or cess pool, was generally shared by many. The epidemics put increasing pressure on Parliament to take action. It came in 1847 when cess pools were abolished in the capital, and in the following year a Health Act ensured that all houses had sanitary provisions. The battle against typhoid and cholera was finally under way.

The confidence and bravado of Victorian builders extended even to this murky, subterranean world. Modern sewers, stark and functional, are built with the attitude that there is no one down there to see them anyway. Little more than a century ago they were built with skill and grandeur as meandering cathedrals with vaulted roofs and impressive pillars, and their creators even signed the finished work. They were marvellous feats of civil engineering, and a major advance in public health. For the first time, the streets were cleaner and the air was sweet – but sewage was still a health hazard, even if it did enter the river further downstream. Once again the Victorians showed their ingenuity and skill. The flow was guided from the cities to sewage works, which became a matter of great civic pride as well as necessity.

The treatment of sewage in Bradford began in 1872, in cleverly designed buildings which concealed their purpose from passers-by. To the casual rambler they presented an agreeable pastoral scene. Some resembled town halls, or small stately homes set in parkland, all displaying the greatest attention to the tiniest architectural detail. More importantly they were effective, turning raw sewage, the dreaded carrier of disease, into virtually harmless waste.

In Bradford, which was the centre of the world's wool trade, there was a curious twist to the tale. As wool was cleaned in dozens of mills across the city, lanolin, a valuable by-product, was washed away. Rather than waste it, sewage was boiled and filtered, and the lanolin recycled and sold for the manufacture of ladies' cosmetics and, ironically, soap. It gave a considerable boost to the growing business of promoting hygiene. The wealthy had used soap since the sixteenth century, when white Castile was imported from Spain. Blocks reeking of olive oil, from Venice and Marseilles, could also be found adorning their bathtubs.

As cleanliness drew nearer to godliness in the years of sanitary reform, Britain's soap boilers prospered. Bristol, well-placed for raw materials, established itself as the nation's soap-making capital, and soon faced strong competition from Coventry. Foul-smelling tallow from Russia and whale oil brought by the tall ships were used to manufacture three standard grades. The most expensive was speckled, followed by white, and the cheapest, an unrefined and uninviting grey.

For almost 150 years a soap tax of up to three pence in the pound had put it beyond the reach of working people, who arguably needed it more than anyone. In 1853 the levy was repealed by Gladstone, losing the Exchequer around one million pounds a year, but providing at a stroke, soap for the people. Victorian penny magazines advertised it widely, and the virtues of cleanliness were a constant theme.

Few of us now reflect on the Victorian's contribution to public health and hygiene. Yet, in the space of 150 years, their efforts helped us to move from the horror of open sewers and vaporous streets to become a relatively healthy nation.

Motives behind the great sanitary reforms were not entirely altruistic – London had become so obnoxious that MPs, sitting alongside the stinking Thames, had to do something to ensure their own survival. Business in the House of Commons was frequently held up because of the smell, and sacks soaked in lime were hung at the windows. Eventually a Parliamentary committee – known as the Smelling Expedition – was forced to investigate the problem. The fight for fresh air which followed was spurred by a fashionable theory among doctors that smells themselves gave rise to fevers, 'effluvia' and 'miasmas'.

The Law Courts was just as bad: 'steam jets' were

A hymn to the water closet – public lavatories were slow to catch on, but soon developed into elaborate affairs.

introduced in the Courts of Exchequer and Common Pleas in 1850, where both plaintiffs and barristers had been known to collapse from the smell. When one senior judge, Sir Thomas Coltman, died in 1849 the cause of his demise was attributed to a prolonged stint at the Old Bailey. The Thames became so insufferable that the Temple and Westminster Hall were closed down as uninhabitable in the hot summer of 1858. Conditions were little better elsewhere – the smell from bad ventilation, exacerbated by nearby cess pits, was so overpowering at Lincoln Crown Court that the judge found himself unable to wait while the usher struggled to open the windows, and ordered the glass to be smashed.

A drawing in Punch in 1849 showed a top-hatted gentleman walking the streets of London wearing a strange gas mask which terminated in a ten-foot stand pipe above his head. It was, the caption explained, to enable the wearer 'to breathe the upper and purer currents of air in the neighbourhood of our slaughterhouses, cattle markets, graveyards, bone-boilers, soapmakers and catgut manufacturers.'

As the cities were successfully cleansed in a concerted campaign of sanitary reform, an equally important change kept pace – the cleaning of the people. In the 1840s sanitary-minded councils began to open public baths where, for a small charge, you could enjoy a hot or cold tub, and also wash the family clothes in the laundry. They were an immediate success, and a pattern began to evolve

ABOVE: *Victorian pumping stations were a wonderful blend of art and engineering. The echoing galleries, stout pillars and gleaming machines at London's Abbey Road are a fine example.*

TOP RIGHT: *Many old civic sewage works house well-preserved examples of Victorian pumping engines, occasionally still in harness.*

BOTTOM RIGHT: *Bradford's sewage works built in 1872, featured cleverly-designed buildings which concealed their purpose from passers-by.*

OPPOSITE RIGHT: *Although unlikely ever to be seen, Victorian sewers contained a wealth of architecture and were a triumph of engineering.*

throughout the country. Fresh water was novelty enough in the cities, but to have clean *hot* water on tap was not only a real achievement, but paradise itself. Without adequate supplies of clean water, it was true to say of the working man that the only time he was well-washed was at the moment of birth and the hour of death.

A few magnificent municipal swimming baths still remain – there is a fine example in Glasgow's North Woodside – but swimming was not their only function. Slipper baths were the Victorian solution to the problem of the great unwashed.

As the name suggests, slipper baths looked like strange pieces of enamelled footwear. Soap was provided in individual cubicles and, for the first time, the common man could return home pink and scrubbed, to find his family equally clean. As an incentive, cheap group rates were offered for children. Many of the early plunge pools – or ponds, as they were called in Glasgow – were communal baths. The pursuit of cleanliness remained a key feature, but swimming was slowly drifting into fashion. New public baths catered for the growing pastime, and what was once a sanitary activity began to emerge as a competitive sport. By the time swimming was introduced into the Olympic Games, in 1896, the emphasis was on keeping the water, not the bather, clean.

There is yet another strand to the story of sanitary reform. When Elizabeth I announced that she took a bath once a month, 'whether I need it or no', she was not referring to the state of her cleanliness. At that time bathing was seen almost solely as a treatment for the sick, and a belief in the healing powers of water went on through the great days of the spas. The rich would arrive to drink and bathe in surroundings as grand and decorative as anything seen since the days of the Romans.

Harrogate has had pump rooms since the eighteenth century, but in the Victorian era it blossomed into an elegant environment in which the genteel could pass the time in splendid gardens, hotels and assembly rooms, while taking the waters. The Royal Baths were completed in 1897, and in August

Swimming became immensely popular after its introduction to the Olympic Games in 1896 – these bathing beauties were among the first to take the plunge.

the following year 52,000 glasses of water were served, and 18,000 baths taken. The famous waters, which gurgled from old sulphur wells, were distinctive to say the least. 'It stinks noisomely, like rotten eggs,' one visitor noted.

'It is curious to observe the various effects these draughts produce on the countenances of those who partake of them,' another wrote. 'Disgust is expressed in a thousand ludicrous ways.' But for the constant stream of Victorian devotees, a belief in the therapeutic qualities of Harrogate water was unshaken.

Swimming pools were usually surrounded by enclosed changing facilities in keeping with the modesty of the day.

Tasting Britain's Spas Today

Bath: The Roman baths are among the best-preserved Roman remains in Britain. Bath has plans to become an internationally popular spa again in an ambitious scheme with a private consortium. The famous waters, turned off in 1983 by health inspectors, are now flowing again.

Buxton: A nineteenth-century spa town nestling in a circle of Derbyshire hills. Spa water still flows from a drinking fountain at the Royal Devonshire Hospital, which was formerly the Pump Room.

Cheltenham: 'Here lies I and my three daughters,
   Died from drinking Cheltenham
   waters.
   If we had stuck to Epsom Salts,
   We shouldn't be lying in these cold
   vaults.'

But despite this inscription on a local tombstone, Cheltenham water remains popular today, cool and clear from a well in the Pitville Pump Room.

Droitwich: Once famous for its brine baths in which the dedicated floated for hours on end. After a decade of decline, the brine baths are opening again.

Harrogate: In days gone by many found the sulphur taste unpalatable and quaffed it with a queasy smile. It can still be tasted in the Royal Pump Museum.

Leamington Spa: A conglomeration of classical architecture surrounds the Pump Room where therapeutic waters can be taken. Thousands swear to their efficacy.

Llandrindod Wells: Refreshing water from springs deep beneath the mountains of Mid Wales. The Victorian Pump Room has been lovingly restored, and is well worth a visit.

Malvern: A thriving bottled water industry exports the subtle taste of Malvern Water to the world. The hilly Victorian town still has springs where visitors can taste it at source.

Strathpeffer: A delightful sandstone Victorian village, laid out by the Duchess of Sutherland, where local highland water flows in the Pump Room.

Tunbridge Wells: Some say the water here is an acquired taste, but all agree that it is rich in iron. Obtainable five days a week in the Pantiles, a beautiful seventeenth-century covered shopping precinct.

Other towns of lesser appeal were swift to recognize the potential of the health spa. A most gallant, if incongruous, effort was made in industrial Wigan where a pump room, shrewdly called New Harrogate House, was opened between the gas works and a dye factory. The location left a little to be desired, but the sulphur spring, discovered by surveyors prospecting for coal, was an unexpected windfall.

In the excitement of a civic opening, accompanied by the strains of a string orchestra and the gentle flap of bunting, it was almost possible to forget that this was the coal capital of Lancashire. A dozen local worthies were persuaded to lay down their dominoes in the parlour of the nearby Dog and Partridge, and grace the occasion with their presence.

Coaches were soon disgorging the well-heeled sick to squat on wooden benches ranged around a twelve-foot square pool, beneath an elegant roof. The partially sighted dabbed the water on their eyes, and swore by its curative properties. Others purchased bottles of Wigan Water to take home and sip at their leisure. Local publicans capitalized on the thriving industry by mixing sulphur water with their spirits. Wigan's glory, however, was short-lived. Seepage from local mineworkings contaminated the spring, and the wealthy disappeared as quickly as they had come. The pump room was demolished and a row of miners' cottages built over it.

Even the splendour of Harrogate fell victim to changing times. The last of the pump rooms closed fifteen years ago, and the sulphur water has now given way to cups of café tea. In its Victorian heyday many water therapies were available, including mud baths, but only one remains, in the form of a magnificent Turkish bath.

The idea of steam baths had been brought with the Crusaders, although it was a short-lived fashion, providing a cloak for bawdy houses. In 1858 they were reintroduced by David Urquhart, traveller, author and friend of Karl Marx. Subsequently came the decor consisting of architectural flights of Moorish fantasy, capturing the mystery of the East. Urquhart's campaigning generated great enthusiasm for Turkish baths among Victorians, who even saw them as a great benefit to animals. ACCIDENT TO HORSE IN TURKISH BATH – A WARNING, the *Irish Times* reported in 1864. The mishap occurred at Carysfort House, when the first four-legged client was led into a Turkish bath specially designed by Urquhart. The horse, the article recorded, 'was with difficulty constrained from destroying himself by the combined efforts of about a dozen men.'

Urquhart, enthusiasm undiminished, went on to build dozens of Turkish baths, including eight for himself – one a 'private sweating closet' at his holiday cottage in Worthing. He constructed Turkish baths for sheep and hens, TB patients at Brompton Consumptive Hospital, and for lunatics at Colney Hatch. All were but a warm-up exercise for his greatest triumph – a 7,000 sq ft building in Jermyn Street, at a cost of £20,000. Among his converts was Sir John Fife, an eminent Victorian surgeon who, in 1847, had visited the first Turkish bath in Britain, in Northumberland, and emerged a purified devotee.

'The pig,' Sir John wrote excitedly, 'is the animal for which I see the greatest benefit from the bath. The sweetening of its flesh, and the restoration of its dimensions are all ensured at a greatly-reduced

Harrogate's Victorian Turkish Baths were designed to capture all the atmosphere of the mysterious East. Customers can still soak up the steam in splendid Moorish surroundings.

expenditure of food.' Victorians, clearly impressed with Turkish baths, could not help but agree. One of Lord Kinnaird's weekly returns from the Turkish bath at his Mill Hill farm read: 'Men, 25; women, 19; horses, 5; pigs, 7; dogs, 4. Total – 60.'

Sir John Fife went on to edit the Manual of the Turkish Bath, in 1865, which became a public declaration of his conviction. 'I state solemnly, as a result of my experiences,' he recorded, 'that the action of the Turkish bath is immediate and direct in the treatment of the ague, barrenness, cancer, cataract, cholera, consumption, dyspepsia, eczema, heart disease, hydrophobia, insanity, insobriety, sprains, stomach disorders, swelling joints and sunstroke.'

Turkish baths – along with Russian baths, swimming pools, and later the ubiquitous sauna – survive today. At the same time however, we have seen the demise of public baths and the splendid, imaginative buildings which housed them. The plunge pools and slipper baths have been neglected, destroyed or replaced by concrete civic swimming baths – and with them an important piece of our irreplaceable heritage has been lost.

FIND OUT FOR YOURSELF

Look for: all the signs of how water was obtained in your community. There may be springs or wells, reservoirs, aqueducts and pumping stations.

* the swimming baths, public wash houses and public conveniences built in the last century. How many have been pulled down in recent years?

* the pride and care that went into Victorian public buildings, particularly the carvings and decorative details.

Reservoirs in which water is collected are worth a second look. They can be remarkable structures built by huge gangs of navvies, living in villages that had the characteristics of the American Wild West. These villages are unlikely to have survived, but you may come across men and women who worked on the reservoirs in your area, and who have more than enough good stories to tell.

A phrase given popularity by the Victorians was 'the great unwashed', and though few public wash houses remain, swimming baths, public conveniences and spas still do. Though we might use the word spa infrequently these days, and associate it only with towns like Harrogate, Leamington and Cheltenham, there were in fact many smaller spas. Indeed, wherever there was a spring of mineral water, there might be a spa. It is worth looking at street names on old maps to see if such a spa existed in your town.

History can be found in the most surprising places, such as sewage works and water stations. They may not be as accessible as the local swimming baths but, in some towns, quite remarkable pumping machinery and early steam engines still exist.

Many of the water authorities have helpful leaflets about such things as amenity use of reservoirs. You can find their number in the local telephone directory – ask to be put through to the public relations department. In some cases there may be a librarian who will be able to help with information on the history of man's use of water in your area. For specific enquiries try: The Information Department
National Water Council
1 Queen Anne's Gate
London SW1H 9BJ.

3

A Taste of History

If shopping, as we know it today, has a birthplace, it is probably Newcastle-upon-Tyne. Like many other fine Victorian cities, it shows its wealth and confidence in its architecture. Grey Street, designed by John Grainger, has been called the most beautiful street in Europe.

Newcastle has existed since Roman times, but Victorians never had much of a regard for the past. A new generation of buildings sprang up to meet the needs of a growing commercial society – a railway station, banks, offices, theatres and, more interestingly, shops. . . . The city has a long marketing tradition, but sadly some of it has had to make way for a modern shopping precinct. Some examples of Newcastle's long tradition of trade can still be seen, including Bainbridge's – the first department store in the world. The French proudly claim that the first department store was Bon Marché, in Paris, but three English department stores were already in business when it opened its doors.

Draper Emerson Bainbridge opened his shop – now called Binn's – in 1841. Five years later he astutely put an end to the common practice of bargaining, and labelled all his goods with a fixed price. By 1849

To the Victorian retailer display was everything. Even this barber shop followed the trend by putting all its equipment on show for the customer's approval.

Department stores boomed in Edwardian times – light, airy structures which displayed all the goods to the best advantage at fixed prices (RIGHT). Along with covered shopping arcades (ABOVE) they took over from outdoor markets to create a shopping revolution. Many have since been demolished to make way for modern city centre developments.

there were twenty-three departments, and business was booming. Department stores were at their peak in relaxed Edwardian times, when customers were offered a seat while being served, and every parcel was wrapped in crackly brown paper and tied with string. Bainbridge's prospered until its departments had spread throughout the entire block, and a whole shopping revolution was born – no bargaining, clearly-priced goods, and freedom to wander around with no obligation to buy.

In 1855 Willey & Lockhead opened a new extension to their department store in Glasgow's Buchanan Street. It was designed around a glass-covered central well, surrounded by elegant glass balconies, to overcome the problem of inadequate gas lighting. For the first time, all the goods could be shown off to their best advantage. Unfortunately, as beautiful as these building are, few survive as they were originally intended.

Liberty's, in London's Regent Street, is an excellent example of the airy light-well style of department store design. This form of shopping, with a variety of departments, is now the province only of a handful of large groups. Today's fashion for the chainstore is a different, and probably less rewarding, shopping experience.

Arcades, too, are sadly decreasing in numbers. In a combination of glass and cast iron, their most advanced building material, Victorian builders created walkways of gossamer beauty. There is a fine example of a restored early Victorian shopping arcade tucked away in a back alley, off St Anne's Square, Manchester. Newcastle has a copy of its original arcade which was pulled down to make way for another planners' dream – the fully integrated urban motorway. When the entire structure was dismantled each stone was carefully numbered and stored in a field. Putting it all back together again proved too complicated for modern engineers. Part of it was used to restore a nearby abbey. With the help of some of the original materials, the arcade was recreated under a modern office block in the middle of a roundabout – surrounded by concrete and carbon monoxide.

The open market is probably the oldest form of shopping, hardy and enduring despite the changes taking place around it. Putting a roof on an open market was the Victorians' contribution to more comfortable shopping. Not quite a department store, but at least it was practical and dry. Many splendid iron and glass affairs still survive, keeping alive the friendly quality of the open market.

The world of supermarkets, hypermarkets and chainstores has replaced the traditional shopping experience and the local corner shop. Every street had one – a meeting place where you knew the owner, goods were fresh, prices were fair and produce free from plastic wrapping. Elsewhere, fresh sea fish lay on marble slabs waiting to be lovingly converted into meals fit for some eminent Victorian. High standards were expected by an increasingly discerning generation. Those with style shunned dinner at home, despite its wholesomeness, and took to eating out. Food was an art, and new restaurants appeared to meet the demand.

The Perfect Marriage

Traditional food, it seems, is really the food of the working man. There have been fish fryers in our towns for several centuries, although for many years they were put on a level with blood boilers because of the smell. There were potato fryers, too, but it was a long time before anyone made the small but significant step of marrying the two.

It finally happened in the East End of London in 1868, and a great convenience food was born – high in calories and protein, cheap and quick. Good solid belly timber to keep people going; the very essence of traditional food. Fish and chips is now a national institution, with few rivals in the growing field of fast convenience foods. It may be served with curry sauce to meet the demands of a more sophisticated market, but the basic product is still with us, unchanged.

Food for the masses: a nourishing plate of eels, pie and mash at Cooke's of Dalston. Live eels ('wobblin' about like walkin' wheels') await the large daily flow of East End customers.

In a recently published survey on established British eating habits, eels and tripe were found rubbing shoulders with Chinese takeaways and curry sauce. The authors concluded that if a dish had been around for ten years, then it was traditional.

When we began our research I felt sure that our eating habits would reveal a rich historical tale – especially the food we eat in restaurants. So what is traditional English food? The immediate answer would be roast beef, salmon and game, but when most of us go out to eat we seem to forget our traditions.

Indian, Chinese, Hungarian, French and Mexican restaurants are almost as plentiful as those preparing English food, and show just how much our palates have changed. Only twenty years ago it would have seemed pretty adventurous and exotic to be eating the foods of the East. And when you do find an

English restaurant selling English meals it is ironic that what was once working man's food, such as oysters, is now at the top of the market. Local popular foods were – and still are – high in calories and low on cost to give lots of energy. In Yorkshire children were told: 'Them who eat most puddin, will get most meat.' Eager children dutifully tucked into two or three Yorkshire puddings, and then found they were not hungry when the more expensive meat dish came along.

In other parts of the country they would make the whole dish in one huge pan, or cauldron. The liquid in which the meat had been cooked would be first served as soup, followed by some kind of dumpling dish. Finally they would come to a tiny piece of meat which had had all the goodness boiled out of it. This type of dish was common in Lincolnshire where, like their Yorkshire counterparts, children would be too full with soup to eat much more.

Fish and chips always taste better from newspaper, but there is an even more traditional way for the working man to wrap his food. The most efficient and filling method of carrying meat to work is in a pie: the Cornish pasty is the perfect edible lunch box.

To some people the pasty is a meal in itself, to others merely a supporting character to the star of the show . . . eels. Whatever your reaction to them, eels are no different to other fish. They are high in protein and, unlike oysters, have not become a rich man's food. Eels can still be found – but only just – in the diet of London's East End.

Eel shops are rare today, but Cooke's of Dalston still survives. When it opened in 1862 it was one of many eel shops around, but Cooke's turned the eel world upside down. Alongside their speciality they served steak pie and mashed potato, creating a new cheap and popular meal, which is still an East End favourite.

The Cookes keep several tons of fresh eels in their shop, where the first job each day is to stun and clean them ready for the steady flow of customers. Once boiled, eels are served either hot with pie and mash, or cold as jellied eels which originated in the East End but strangely never travelled further.

Fred and Chris Cooke are third generation Dalston eel sellers. In their grandparents' day eels arrived from Holland daily in heavily-laden barges up the Thames.

Today's eels arrive live at Cooke's from Ireland in the summer months, and New Zealand in the winter. The journey from storage tank to table, including cleaning and boiling, takes just forty-five minutes. American fried chicken and kebabs may nowadays have more appeal for young people, but on Saturdays there is still a queue right out of the door.

Tripe, the traditional dish from Lancashire, is another convenience food in danger. There are still several tripe shops to be found in the North West,

Many Victorian shops, though rich in choice, were superseded by the arrival of the department store and its food halls.

the customers mainly elderly with a lifelong taste for it. Many young people have never sampled tripe, and perhaps don't even know that it is the lining of a cow's stomach. Honeycomb tripe is eaten with salads in the North, while in Birmingham and London they prefer it cooked. Hospitals still order tripe for patients with delicate stomach conditions, because of its reputation for being nutritious and easy to digest.

In an attempt to woo new customers one of

Lancashire's biggest shops hands out printed tripe recipes, most of them with French names. One of them, deep fried diced tripe fritters, tastes a little like scampi; but even Lancashire tripe with a French accent seems unlikely to halt the decline of what was once a traditional British food enjoyed by thousands.

Soyer's lamb cutlets reforme are still prepared in the kitchens of London's Reform Club.

We have an inferiority complex about our own cuisine. There is a general feeling that British food is rather dull, and that anyone else's is preferable, however bad it may seem. Oddly, one of the reasons for this self-deprecating outlook may be found amongst London's gentlemans' clubs. The Reform Club, for instance, boasted a French chef from the day it first opened in 1841. He was Alexis Soyer, and one of the great dishes he created, lamb cutlets reforme, is still cooked in the kitchens today.

Edward Ellis, the club's founder, was the Whig party whip at the time of the Reform Bill crisis. He realized that the way to bond the different factions that were to become the Liberal Party was with good food which he discovered proved to be 'a powerful agent of political cohesion'. Lamb cutlets reforme is not the only legacy the remarkable emigré chef left to the club – his influence was to spread half way round the world. When Soyer joined the Reform he was paid £1000 a year, a pound for every member which in the 1840s was a small fortune.

He personally designed the kitchens in collaboration with the club's architect Sir Charles Barry. 'They are as spacious as a ballroom, as white as a young bride,' one commentator enthused. It was here that Soyer held court, receiving visitors, preparing banquets and attending to arrangements for marketing his sauce. Work outside the club was equally demanding. He ran soup kitchens for the poor and, in 1855, travelled to the Crimea to organize field kitchens for the army and reformed the military catering system singlehanded.

Conditions in the Crimea were appalling. Troopers had to wrap a joint of meat in an old sock to prove it was theirs before they dropped it in the cauldron. When they brought it out, they threw the water away. This, Soyer found unbelievable – he saved the water and collected ox heads and tails, which soldiers had previously buried as useless, and made soups. He also invented a portable cooking stove, designed to maintain a steady heat, which the British army was still using 100 years later. Back at the Reform Club, catering for a rich and wasteful society, Soyer still saved every morsel – a characteristic of French cooking at its best. Whether he was cooking for soldiers, down-and-outs or millionaires, it made no difference – Soyer applied his skill unstintingly to every aspect of his life and work. His kitchen, though much smaller now, is still in use. And the high standards he began are maintained along with his famous dish.

Soyer sauce, which is the centrepiece of lamb cutlets reforme, has an interesting history because it is not particularly French. It is highly spiced with a taste of chilli and vinegar, ideally suited to the palates of club members who had returned from India. In a single sauce Soyer cleverly united several centuries of national taste.

One person who regrets the diminishing influence of Soyer is former Good Food Guide editor Christopher Driver. For the price of the guide anyone can contribute an opinion about a restaurant, and help good establishments to keep on going.

'One man, with his own very high standards, united the best, most expensive recherché dishes you could invent with the completely popular and cheapest possible, in the economic sense. When he took his vast cauldron to the soup kitchens and cooked for the starving, he did it to the same high standards of the Reform Club. What has happened now – and what the Good Food Guide has drawn attention to for over thirty years – is that these two things are blown apart.' Caring about the quality of food is no less worthy than caring about the more tangible examples of the past. If we do not show our concern, then food is going to become little more than pre-packed manufacturers' substitutes which do not taste the same, no matter what they claim.

'The people who are making the money selling rubbish in packets and tins would never be seen dead tasting it – and, in most cases, that's why it tastes that way,' Driver says.

'It is the contempt implicit in the way in which people are treated that makes me angry. It is assumed that nobody knows, that nobody has cooked themselves, that nobody can taste the difference. I'm afraid that a lot of the problem, too, is the fault of the customers. They do not make comparisons for themselves, or within their families, and communicate their judgments to the man in the restaurants or the manager in the supermarket who

The last resting place of Alexis Soyer – the dishes he created live on.

is responsible for what he is selling.'

Perhaps the problem is not that we are bad communicators, just that we do not like complaining. But there have been successful complainers – the Campaign for Real Ale, for instance; and, thanks to a loaf lobby, bread has risen from its ghostly white sick-bed to become more wholesome. Those, of course, are the exceptions. Many foods are simply disappearing, and more are sure to follow. We have societies for the protection of ancient buildings, but few for the protection of British cheese, for example. Such things can change before our eyes and palates before we have hardly noticed. In many places it is easier to buy a pound of kiwi fruit from the greengrocer, than it is to purchase a pound of good British peas in their season. Fish becomes a frozen slab, Cheddar cheese is manufactured in an immense block instead of on truckles where it properly matures. Ham is rarely cured traditionally, and is quite frequently injected with water to increase its value per pound. The production of Lancashire cheese, one of Britain's finest cheeses, is currently confined to about six farms who make it in the proper way. Substitutes do not taste the same, and if we are not vigilant about the ordinary things we buy each week, they simply disappear.

FIND OUT FOR YOURSELF

Good Food Guide
14 Buckingham Street
London WC2N 6DS.
Dedicated to preserving standards of good, reasonably-priced eating.

Business Archives Council
15 Tooley Street
London SE1 2PN.
The BAC has promoted the study of Britain's industrial and commercial history for half a century, and answers specific research questions. A stamped addressed envelope is a great help.

The Archivist
John Lewis PLC
Cavendish Road
Stevenage SG1 2EH
Hertfordshire.

Company Archivist
House of Fraser PLC
69 Buchanan Street
Glasgow G1 2LE.

The Librarian
Debenhams PLC
1 Welbeck Street
London W1A 1DF.

Company Archivist
J. Sainsbury PLC
Stamford House
Stamford Street
London SE1 9LL.

All are pleased to receive enquiries in writing on company history and the development of the department store. Sainsbury's and the House of Fraser have a number of leaflets available on request.

4

GREAT GARDENS OF SLEEP

Wherever you live, one of the most accessible sources of history is not more than a short walk away – in the local cemetery. One of the richest examples, the Necropolis – literally the city of the dead – stands high above the busy hubbub of Glasgow, very much a city of the living. The monuments of the Necropolis appear clean-cut and hard-edged against the skyline. It is perhaps Britain's finest cemetery, an imposing jumble of classical harmony and precision, designed to be visited.

Originally a private cemetery, it was founded by the Merchants' House (an association of merchants) in 1828 on land owned by them and was opened in 1833. The intention was that people should wander at leisure along carefully-planned terraces and recall the virtues of the departed. A monument to the cemetery's creator John Knox was erected prior to its opening in 1825. The Necropolis has a unique quality, which once led it to be described as the Westminster Abbey of Glasgow. One visitor, John Lauden, noted in 1841 that even from a distance, 'there appeared to be no mean, trivial or vulgar form among its monuments.' The comparative newness of the sculpted hill overlooking the city suggests an elegant solution to a particularly melancholic, if not gruesome problem. The earliest cemeteries began in the 1820s, even the Necropolis is only 150 years old, so what did people do with their dead before then?

There was a time when everyone used to be buried either in church or in the churchyard. There were no hard and fast regulations about the depth and spacing of graves but everyone maintained the unwritten rule of laying the deceased facing east. Clergymen were interred in the opposite direction, facing west. The idea was that when the final day of judgment came, everyone would rise up facing Jerusalem and all the clerics would be in a natural position to address their congregations.

'Since mankind began to leave traces of his civilizations, death has exercised his mind to no small degree,' says Dr James Stevens Curl, architectural historian and an expert on funeral sculpture. 'It is the only certainty, for everything that is born must die. This fact has contributed to man's desire to commemorate his fleeting existence on earth by building monuments, erecting funerary architecture, and otherwise celebrating death.'

Exton Parish Church, Rutland, has a great range of ecclesiastical sculpture and architecture from the middle ages to the eighteenth century.

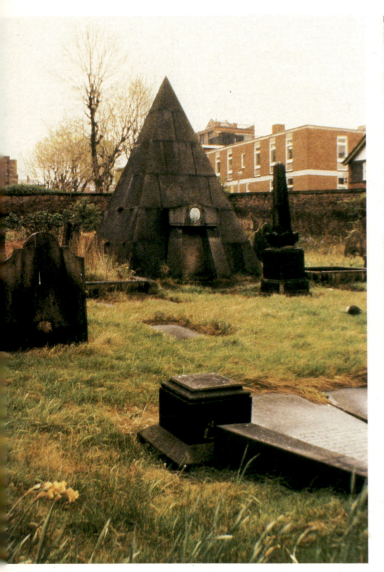

ABOVE: *Lest we forget . . . a bizarre pyramidal resting place in a Church of Scotland graveyard, Liverpool.* TOP RIGHT: *Dr James Stevens Curl in the land of the green marble chips.* BOTTOM RIGHT: *Dr James Stevens Curl in the splendour of Bottesford Church.*

In the Middle Ages, prayers for the dead were an essential part of religious devotion. Large sums of money were paid to ensure that they were chanted for the souls of the departed. These observances were known as chantries, and the rich and great had chantry chapels built over their burial places. They were often ornate and canopied, like miniature churches within churches. Winchester cathedral contains some of the finest examples in Europe, enclosed by stone screens of delicate tracery.

In time the unpalatable, physical facts of death crept into funerary art with giant effigies, intended to remind the living that death is the great leveller. Church sculptors chiselled away with macabre relish at graphic representations of the realities of decay. An example at Winchester is the effigy of the decomposing body of Bishop Fox who died in 1528. The corpse lies collapsed and shrinking, with bones protruding beneath the tightening skin. In Chesterfield, an extraordinary series of monuments

The beauty of the English country church . . . Bottesford Parish Church, Leicestershire, has a wealth of stonework and fine architecture.

show death, old age and childhood with bones, shovels and a figure in a shroud . . . not a smirking angel in sight.

Nothing is more closely associated with England than the local church, standing in the centre of a town or village, its spires and towers dominating the landscape. Each is unique – fashioned from local materials, evolving over the centuries and reflecting the fortunes of bygone times. Churches, with their stained glass, carved roofs, medieval altars and the glorious sound of a well-trained choir, are loved and enjoyed and are a vast museum accessible to all. They delight the eye and stimulate the mind with what is possibly the greatest collection of sculpture in the world. When it comes to the churchyard however, we scurry through with little more than a second glance. Strangely, an interest in tombstones and funerary monuments is often dismissed as morbid.

Death can be terrible, glorious, or merely commonplace. In Bottesford Church, Leicestershire –

43

architecturally at least – it can hardly be described as ordinary. The tiny chancel has a clutter of monuments commemorating the death of no less than eight earls. They block the view of the altar in a log-jam of bombast – a memorial to a rich, confident, pushy society, unencumbered by tiresome notions of self-effacement or good works.

Bottesford, with its rich range of stones, both inside and out, is a favourite of Dr James Stevens Curl. 'How much more suitable are many of the traditional gravestones as a setting for the church,' he says, 'than the inappropriate marbles that dissolve in our damp, acidic atmosphere.

'Certain modern memorials, headstones, stone borders and – horror of horrors – green chips have added new terrors to death. They do nothing for the character of the churchyard, save reduce it to the level of a gnome-filled garden, or a sanctuary for bird-baths.

'The clearances of churchyards are perpetrated by those who wish to tidy, who wish to pretend things are not what they are, and who think that churchyards were never used as burial places,' he says.

'Death is not a tidy thing. I believe that we have no right to destroy memorials – they are examples of craftsmanship, design, the taste of many periods, and often all that survives to remind us of many a humdrum life.'

For several centuries churchyards were periodically cleared as they became full, and the bones of the dead stored in charnel houses. In some places the dead were buried on top of older graves. However, when the population began to increase in the early nineteenth century, city churchyards could no longer cope. It was quite literally a grave problem. In London, for example, the amount of burial space in the 1820s had not increased at all since medieval times. Forty-four thousand people a year had to be interred, and it quite simply could not be done. One or two late eighteenth-century churches had been built with large burial vaults beneath them, but they were strictly parochial and not for the use of families outside the area.

A solution had to be found and plots of land were commissioned outside towns and cities for cemeteries – the first in Britain were in Belfast and Scotland. Despite this the problem was finally solved by private enterprise, but share-holding cemetery companies took more than thirty years to achieve any kind of headway.

Dr James Stevens Curl, and friend.

Liverpool, a leader in sanitary reform, led the way in England by opening its first cemetery in 1825. It was quite small, about the size of Anfield football pitch, but during the next four years a more ambitious cemetery was developed in a nearby quarry. Architect John Foster created a dramatic setting, with processional ramps and tunnels carved through solid sandstone to give unexpected views. It had a refreshing, pastoral atmosphere. The greatest tomb belongs to MP William Huskisson, who accidentally stepped in front of the inaugural train from Manchester to Liverpool, becoming the world's first rail accident victim.

If sanitary reform was desirable in Liverpool, it was essential in London. As early as the 1820s people had been wondering how to dispose of their dead. There had been futuristic schemes for an enormous cemetery at Primrose Hill, so ambitious that it proved impossible to build. Others ranged from vast underground networks of catacombs, to a gigantic pyramid outside the city walls capable of housing five

Liverpool's great garden of sleep, St James' necropolis, one of the first public cemeteries in the country. It was designed on a grand scale by architect John Foster.

Derby Road Necropolis, Liverpool, the city's first cemetery. Laid out in 1825, it set a trend for public burial throughout Britain.

million dead. About half a dozen private cemeteries sprang up, each consisting of about two or three acres.

These were followed by a handful of enterprising burial chapels. In one of the most infamous the proprietor, who appointed himself minister, spent nine years cramming 12,000 corpses into a basement 18 m by 12 m (60 ft by 40 ft). The upstairs room, where services were held, unfortunately did not have a tongue and groove floor and an obnoxious smell filtered through. Eventually it had to be closed down.

George Carden, a barrister, had tried to do something about this rather pressing concern by writing articles to leading journals about the state of burials in England. In 1825, after a well-attended public meeting, he formed the London Cemetery Company.

Charles Dickens described London in the 1830s as a city that smelled of mildew and decomposition, and by most contemporary accounts it was pretty foul. When a widespread cholera epidemic hit London at this time, the situation became more desperate, and eight private cemeteries were developed in the suburbs to help ease the problem.

Kensal Green Cemetery was one of these, and was the first venture of the London Cemetery Company. It was sited on the bank of the Grand Union Canal, and early plans included a lock gate for water-borne funerals. The grounds were planted with trees and laid out in serpentine walks. Kensal Green arrived socially with the interment of both the Duke of Sussex and Princess Sophia, children of George III. The duke refused to be buried at Windsor because of the smell.

Kensal Green today is still enchanting, despite the fact that, in common with many of Britain's burial places, pathways have been filled with green and blue-chipped modern graves, and the original landscaping has changed beyond recognition. Perhaps the greatest step forward, however, came in 1850 when the Metropolitan Interment Act closed down London's unhygienic and overcrowded burial places.

Cemeteries were part of a growing movement in public hygiene that radically improved the health of towns and cities, making it possible to live without fear of contagion, or of being moved after death. Whole families would walk in the new cemeteries on Sundays to improve their knowledge of architecture, sculpture, botany and arboriculture, while reflecting on the realities of death and the peaceful beauty of the 'sleeping place'.

Memorials vandalized, gravestones overgrown – the unhappy fate of Victorian urban cemeteries today.

Everything progressed in an orderly manner until the ever-increasing population of the capital began to outpace the reforms and, by the 1880s, the burial situation began to look very much like the 1820s all over again. Then, as if by divine intervention, a new solution appeared – the crematorium. Traditional fashions of disposing the dead slowly changed and the problems which necessitated great cemeteries – such as Highgate created in 1838 by the London Cemetery Company, were never seen again.

Cemeteries of the nineteenth century offer us an immense legacy of landscapes and architecture. Commentators thought them to be educational, morally uplifting, and generally an improving agency for the masses – they were civilized and civilizing places. This point of view is sadly ignored by the vandals and developers who attempt to tear them down.

Bradford's Undercliffe Cemetery, which opened in 1854, is a fine example of the many private and public enterprises established when indecently overcrowded burial grounds were being closed down. It was noted as one of the most striking and beautiful features of the town – 'a favourite place of resort for the inhabitants'. That symbol of the power and prosperity of nineteenth-century industrial Bradford now stands overgrown, broken and vandalized on a bleak and windy hilltop. Just twenty years before it was built, Bradford was little more than a village. It was soon to grow into a bustling city where merchants came to trade from all over the world. Undercliffe expresses its success, and the leaning gravestones and moss-covered mausoleums reflect many a rags-to-riches story.

A complete cross-section of society was laid to rest there. Not just the merchants and manufacturers, the bankers and even the architects who designed the tombs themselves, but the offbeat and unusual too – the keeper of marionettes, and the keeper of theatres lie beside them. They can all justly be regarded as founders of a city which grew from obscurity to become the wool capital of the world in the space of fifty years. Striking examples of family pride, such as a great granite mausoleum in pure Egyptian style, can be found rubbing shoulders with imposing monuments commemorating commercial and political achievement. Cemeteries like Undercliffe have real worth, containing information to be found nowhere else, yet many remain forgotten, untended and unprotected.

Disposing of the dead posed a major problem – the bodies were removed from their homes, sometimes to be stacked in private cellars because of lack of space.

Grave Responsibilities

Undertakers began to appear as a profession in the seventeenth century. They were summoned to remove the deceased from his house and take him off to the cabinet-maker, to be put in his inner coffin. The corpse was then hauled to the plumber where a price was negotiated to have it wrapped in lead. From there the corpse had to be transported to the upholsterer, where another deal had to be struck to have the velvet and fittings supplied. There was a growing need for experienced middlemen to 'undertake' these complicated negotiations on behalf of the bereaved.

Funerals in Victorian times were the last great status symbol, and tremendous social importance was attached to them. An eminent member of the middle classes would have a hearse drawn by four black-plumed horses, with half a dozen or more attendants holding small batons walking on either side, following the undertaker and the mourning coaches. At the front of the hearse there was often a man who solemnly marched with a tray of feathers on his head, flanked by two mutes whose job was to open doors. When the deceased left his home for the last time, he was taken down the street at a leaden march. However, once round the corner the undertaker's lads would smartly unhook the velvet drapes from the horses, throw them on top of the hearse and set off at a brisk pace. Belgian high-steppers were the most popular horses for those who could afford them. They pranced along cobbled streets pulling the swaying hearse, until they reached the cemetery gates. Then the lads would jump off, spread the velvet drapes on the horses again, and lead in the assembled procession at a dignified pace.

If the deceased had a family mausoleum, he usually had not one but three coffins. The first was plain and craftsman-made in elm. It was then wrapped in a lead shell and soldered up with a lead name-plate screwed to the lid. The whole extravagant package was then placed in an oak shell, often up to two inches thick, covered in rich crimson velvet panels. The sides were upholstered and fitted with elaborate silver or brass grip plates, and the lid capped with an enormous breast-plate bearing the name of the deceased.

How unlike today when we are likely to be collected in a Ford Cardinal, whisked into the crematorium on something resembling a Tesco shopping trolley and ultimately disappear into the flames to taped organ music; twenty minutes later, everyone goes home. So how did our attitude to funerals change so drastically?

'Two world wars had a great effect,' explains Julian Litten, of the Victoria and Albert Museum. 'In the nineteenth century death was a welcome guest to the aged and infirm. During the great wars it became a violent intruder and snatcher of the young. And it began to present a great burden to families. They simply could not afford the elaborate funerals of former years.

'Sad to say, the majority did not have the bodies, either – they were left in France or where they had fallen. Much of the demise of the whole panoply also had a lot to do with the introduction of the motor hearse in the 1920s.

'By the end of World War I there were not many horses available, because thousands had been commandeered for military service. The American motor hearse, as it was called, was already popular across the Atlantic, and leading undertakers were anxious to have the latest form of transport in their garages.'

London's Secret Garden

Highgate Cemetery, in North London, is cared for and protected but sadly, because of vandalism, is almost permanently closed to the public. It has become a beautiful yet secret garden, gently decaying behind rusting gates and high walls. Yet Highgate was built to be seen. When it opened, almost 150 years ago, it offered, according to William Justin's guide:

'Winding paths leading through long avenues of cool shrubbery and marble monuments with majestic trees casting broad shadows. Its popular attraction is the combination of Victorian history, architecture and animal and plant life, offering a first rate ramble.'

In its first year of business, Highgate had 204 burials. Such was the excellence of its monuments and landscaping that it soon acquired – along with higher funeral charges – a particular and merited prestige. Plots were sold quite early – one of the early customers was General Sir Loftus Orthway, who commissioned a tomb emblazoned with cannons inverted, big enough to accommodate fifty people. Many monuments were chosen from catalogues, others doggedly individual in cast iron, or reminiscent of St Pancras station. Spaces in the main avenues were sold off to raise money, but cremation and a change in social attitudes hastened its financial decline. In 1975, after already going through one change of ownership, the gates were closed and chained.

Highgate was an effective solution to a particularly unpleasant social problem. If two world wars had not intervened and changed people's approach to death, it would probably still be in business today. Its closing, however, saw the birth of the Friends of Highgate Cemetery, a group of volunteers dedicated to conserving its monuments and wildlife. Their heroic commitment is to secure it as an environmental amenity for the nation.

'All we can do is arrest the rate of decay of the buildings,' says Jean Pateman, secretary of Friends of Highgate. 'But, if people care enough, there is no reason why it should not remain as a nature reserve, or indeed as a burial ground for ever more.

'Highgate is important because it is a significant and beautiful landscaped site. After all, it is the burial ground of 166,000 people, many of whom were very famous. But even those who weren't are worthy of a little tender regard.'

Friends of Highgate are attempting the formidable task of recording every inscription on each of the 51,000 memorials. Valuable information has even come in from overseas. A letter from France, for instance, mentioned that Queen Victoria's midwife was buried there, information which would otherwise have been lost. Lack of money caused Highgate to close, and the same problem has dogged the small band of volunteers dedicated to keeping it open. A Prince of Wales award for services to the community brought in a welcome £1000; the Friends, meanwhile, are ambitiously trying to raise a million.

'In terms of what is now happening in society, I think there is a much greater desire to see a certain reverence for our burial places,' says Jean Pateman. 'It is a strange swing of the pendulum. We are a pioneer exercise for what, I hope, is going on in other areas of Britain.'

Highgate like most of Britain's abandoned cemeteries, is a rich repository of history, providing a fascinating insight into the ephemera of mourning. To stroll its overgrown walkways is to take a privileged peep into the Victorian way of death. Hearses once toiled up the steep hill through arches built just at the right height to allow the nodding plumes of the horses to pass unruffled. The coffin would then have been deposited in its correct mausoleum – a masterpiece of organization in the teeming city of the departed.

There were, of course, those who died before their monument was completed and in the unhurried precision of Highgate, every eventuality was provided for. Among the terraced catacombs, shelves were provided for around ten pounds, where the deceased could wait until the living completed the necessary construction work. Another service was held when the coffin was transferred to its final resting place. Others, for reasons of finance, chose to remain in one of the 5,000 individual loculi housed in the catacombs – worthies and semi-worthies side by side, each with their own inscription. Extravagant memorials abound: Mrs Henry Wood, author of East Lynne, lies under a delightful Grecian day bed; George Rommel, menagerist, beneath a tomb topped by his famous lions. It has been claimed that his coffin was made from the pole which held up his bell tent.

All human life lies in the living sculpture gallery of Highgate. Trades and occupations inscribed on tombstones reveal which professions were the wealthiest. The most important people however, did not necessarily have the most elaborate monuments, so it is interesting, too, to see who were the most pompous. But does it all really matter?

Julian Litten believes it does: 'In a hundred years' time Highgate will be twice as important as it is now. By the time it is 300 years old, it will be of national importance, and its safety concretely guaranteed.

'Provided the wolf can be kept away from the gates, and the Friends of Highgate make sure it is cared for and loved, then it will survive. . .'

Many old churches are painstakingly restored by craftsmen, but the cost of highly-skilled restoration is often prohibitive. As a result churches throughout Britain are slowly deteriorating.

FIND OUT FOR YOURSELF

Friends of Highgate Cemetery
5 View Road
Highgate
London N6 4DJ.

Secretary Jean Pateman will be pleased to give details of restoration work, membership and guided tours.

The Victorian Society
1 Priory Gardens
Bedford Park
London W4.

The Society's recent Cemeteries Survey is full of helpful hints on what to look for when exploring cemeteries, together with a report on the state of them today and what we can do to keep them in good order.

Parish Church of SS Peter & Paul
Exton
Rutland.
All Britain's churches are well worth visiting, and many are of great historical importance. Exton is a fine example, with sculpture from the Middle Ages to the eighteenth century.

5

HANGING ON TO HISTORY

It is a sad fact of modern life that we often throw away what, in a year or two, might be financially invaluable. We demolish buildings which, with a little thought, we would recognize as historically or architecturally significant. Historians do not willingly see their books and manuscripts neglected and destroyed, and yet such things happen to our architectural inheritance.

Facing every one of us now perhaps is a new responsibility to watch out for buildings threatened by the bulldozer's blade, or the town planner's demolition proposals. Not only grand historic buildings, but humble ones – from cafés to covered markets – each splendid and individual, disappear in the name of progress. Repair, unfortunately, is not always possible. Weston-super-Mare's magnificent diving boards were lost, along with the imposing Firestone factory building, in the last few years. Ironically, both were listed. Will future generations wonder who permitted the destruction of the Euston Arch, or the countless other less well-known but equally worthy examples?

The high street was once a glorious jumble of little shops jostling with grand department stores. A few small shops still remain but many were demolished in the planning madness of the 1960s which literally changed the urban face of Britain.

Progress, we are told, is to destroy the old and unnecessary. But is progress nothing more than novelty, uniformity and conformity and does it have to demand such sacrifices? It is easy to be sentimental about the past and the people, rich and poor, who left their mark on the land. The houses they lived in and the places where they worked and worshipped are all their real and hopefully lasting memorial.

Ken Powell, of Save Britain's Heritage, believes that the regret of many people may finally be turning to anger, and that war against the supposedly out-worn is a fading campaign. 'The 1960s and early 1970s were a kind of watershed when people became convinced that progress had its disadvantages and must be controlled,' he says. 'Progress is all very well and good as long as someone has clear and logical control over it – but recent movement has been towards development for development's sake. We carved out ring roads, we threw up office blocks, and we tore down Victorian markets, churches, chapels and houses by the thousand.

'We rebuilt large areas of our cities like Liverpool, Glasgow, Bradford, Leeds and parts of inner London. Then suddenly we found that they did not work very well and it became necessary to adopt a more delicate approach. Conservationists argue that we should make use of our assets and our resources, not throw them down the drain. Optimum use must be made of the products of our greatest age. We cannot just destroy them, grind them into the dust and use them as hardcore for redevelopment.'

Glasgow is one of the growing number of cities now trying to hang on to history with an ambitious programme for its Victorian tenements. Some were in poor condition and had to be replaced, but those that remain are becoming increasingly desirable residences. They are convenient and close to the city centre, homely, spacious and good to look at.

The tenement's greatest asset was its flexibility of design, enabling it to cope with a wide range of needs, from the single person to the large family. What many regarded as a hangover from nineteenth-century urban expansion, is now seen as one of the most successful solutions to the housing problem.

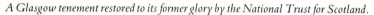
A Glasgow tenement restored to its former glory by the National Trust for Scotland.

Anatomy of Tenement

A typical tenement, built around 1890, is an early and efficient form of system-built housing.

'There was the old-fashioned grate, the pantry and the sink and washboard, which many housewives still remember,' explains Gordon Borthwick, of the National Trust for Scotland. 'Once a week the coalman would deliver a bag of coal, much to her disgust, as she would have to do her dusting all over again. They were built to a standard layout, and someone who had lived in one tenement all their life could go to another and find everything in the same order. In the poorest type, a family would live in one room, with an outside toilet. Others had a parlour, used only for funerals and christenings. Glasgow's top inner city tenements had a parlour, kitchen, bedroom and – the crème de la crème – a built-in-bathroom.'

The National Trust for Scotland became interested in one such tenement which had remained unchanged for half a century. The lady who lived there fell ill and went into hospital but continued to pay her rent. When she died her home and all its contents rested undisturbed – a complete and tiny time capsule. Today her collection of everyday household items has become an increasingly valuable glimpse into the past. Some, such as the Bridgewater bath brick, reflect the ingenuity of forgotten manufacturers. It could be used for cleaning knives and brasses, scouring floors and soaked in paraffin became an 'everlasting' firelighter. Along with another common kitchen utensil – an all-in-one spoon measure marked out for teaspoons, tablespoons and dessert spoons – few modern products show such versatility. Every Glasgow tenement would also own a formidable red box of Gregory Powder which was issued liberally to constipated children.

Two sides of tenement life – the parlour (ABOVE)*, used for christenings and funerals, and the cramped confines of the washroom* (TOP RIGHT)*.*

BOTTOM RIGHT: *Life in a Glasgow tenement – the wall bed was at one time declared illegal when some residents fitted cupboard doors to hide them. Several people suffocated as a result.*

Like many other cities, Glasgow has suffered from the clamours of the knock-it-down brigade, and is rightly proud of its preserved tenement – a unique addition to the National Trust for Scotland's array of glens and castles. According to Gordon Borthwick, it is nothing new for Glasgow: 'When our cathedral was under siege at the time of the Reformation, the Provost of the city appealed to the mob: "Don't knock it down until we have built a better one." As a result Glasgow cathedral remains one of the most important pre-Reformation buildings in the city. If only that legend was invariably engraved in gold above every town hall and planning department in the country. . . .'

Rotherhithe, on London's waterfront presents two very different faces – schemes of careful restoration are now breathing life back into the community.

Four hundred miles south of Glasgow, on the banks of the Thames stands Rotherhithe, wind-blown and decrepit. Many of its old buildings, a mournful reminder of its previous prosperity are suspended in neglect – an infant wasteland waiting to turn into a wilderness.

The scene is not unique to Rotherhithe. In countless areas all over the country people have been moved to distant flats from streets they have lived in for generations. Rotherhithe however is becoming increasingly concerned with the past and what can usefully be done with it. Old warehouses and homes are being converted and renovated, and businesses are developing to meet new demands. Many buildings have changed their use but at least remain intact to give the area its appeal. Rotherhithe is becoming a purposeful indicator of a way in which a whole area can be regenerated; where history is cherished, and development is sympathetic to people's needs, and a stroll around the streets offers a wide variety of experience. The Mayflower public house, for instance, named after the Pilgrim Father's famous ship which took them to America. It was from here that Gulliver was supposed to have set sail. History can be seen too, in Brunnel's newly restored pump house, and around the corner in an eighteenth-century charity school. Nearby, the churchyard of St Mary's has also been saved – all through the efforts of local people. Proof that not only buildings, but a whole area can be made useful again.

But are there enough people who care for the nuts and bolts of history? In a sane society creativity and respect for tradition should be delicately balanced. It is an uneasy relationship between the planner and the preserver. History is not just architecture – it is cemeteries, pubs, packaging, photographs, shops and the food we eat. For many of us history is strictly a wet weather experience, safely locked away in the glass cases of our local museum. But for those who care to look it is easy to see how much information about the past is still around – and how quickly it is disappearing. If we care about our links with history we have to look after them. The future depends upon whether or not we have a sense of the past as well as of the present.

Blackpool businessman John Spencer discovered it in a bundle of maps, diaries and photographs which belonged to his great-grandfather, Benjamin Spencer a Bradford schoolmaster. He was born in 1835 into a world which, thanks to John's presence of mind, can still be explored. Benjamin meticulously recorded, in remarkable detail, every aspect of life for the ordinary families who lived around him. He walked and talked, noting what people ate, how they celebrated Christmas, how much they earned and what they spent it on.

'On Easter Sunday,' he recorded, 'there was no harmonium because of the lack of hymn books and the inability of very many to read. The parson read out two lines of each hymn. There was hymn singing, recitation and a 15-minute sermon. The Yorkshire dialect was freely used.'

'Unless something like a book, or a drama series, is based around Benjamin's records, they will be returned to the archive,' John says wistfully. 'My archive, that is. Because there is not, to my knowledge, a national repository for material of this nature, which is a great pity. . . .'

John Spencer's find was clearly exceptional. We cannot all expect to have an ancestor as observant and prolific as Benjamin, but we all have documents in our homes. It may only be grandmother's ration book, or our first school report, but remember we are not just looking back on history – we are making it too.

John's squirrel instinct saved a piece of conveniently and neatly packaged social history but the past is not always so nicely wrapped. The rolling hills around Huddersfield for instance, are untouched and undamaged and a favourite haunt of Sunday motorists. Popular though it is, the familiar landscape is often overlooked and everyday history blends unnoticed into the scenery. Historian Dr George Redmans decided to breathe life into it again by showing local people their own locality through fresh eyes. He leads conducted bus tours through textile villages, pointing out windows set high in cottages to give weavers adequate light, and the stones from which buildings were constructed.

'I want to put my energy into raising a level of awareness,' he says. 'To create around Huddersfield a climate of public opinion which will enable a vast mass of buildings to survive, or be re-used. In the last 400 years a new landscape has been created in which stone dominates. To me it is a landscape full of character and one that is worth preserving. I think there are ways in which we can achieve that without in any way turning it into a museum.'

To George Redmans it has become a crusade, spreading the word to as many people as possible, encouraging them to appreciate their environment and to ultimately help save it.

'We have had some tragic losses locally,' he recalls. 'Looking back, we could have organized conservation groups to save some of the things which have been pulled down because that sort of thing generally only happens in a world where people do not care.'

But however hard we try to save the obvious there will always be something which slips through the net. Mills and factories are falling to the demolition hammer all over Britain, and occasionally – before anyone realizes it – they may prove to be the last of a forgotten line. Dixon's bobbin mill is an instance of a nineteenth-century factory which supplied wooden bobbins to the world's textile industries. As plastic took over, the workforce dwindled from several hundred to only half a dozen. Demand for their wood-turning skills, which fostered generations of carpenters and joiners steadily fell. Bradford's conservation officer Arthur Saul, and his colleagues

The last days of Dixon's bobbin mill – the end of an industry never to be seen again.

began to work against the clock, recording the remnants of an industry which would simply disappear forever, its workers paid off, buildings boarded up and its ancient equipment sold off.

'Such places tended to be the focal point of the community,' he says. 'Over a period of time the lives of generation after generation were encapsulated in them. The mill was more than just a place of work. It became a social centre, a place around which so many things revolved and evolved. Discovering Dixon's bobbin mill was rather like coming across a dodo. It is a part of the textile industry which we thought had long ceased to exist. It is rather sad that due to the economic situation it finally died. If we had not recorded the process of making wooden bobbins it would be as completely lost as the making of a Roman chariot, disappearing completely into history without recall.'

On 18 January 1983, Dixon's closed its gates for the last time, and the contents were labelled and sold. The only record of its place in history is Arthur Saul's photographs and notes. . . .

FIND OUT FOR YOURSELF

Look out for notices of planning applications in your local paper – these can be the first warnings of important changes.

* threats to historical buildings and sites which may be mentioned in your local press.
* the implications of new road developments. Road planners do not always know what is important to a community's heritage.
* campaigns to save threatened buildings and historical sites.

Ancient Monuments Society
St Andrew-by-the-Wardrobe
Queen Victoria Street, London EC4V 5DE.
Concerned with the study of ancient monuments and historic buildings, with a particular interest in vernacular architecture and churches.

The Civic Trust
17 Carlton House Terrace, London SE17 5AW.
The Civic Trust provides information, and acts as a co-ordinating agency, for one thousand societies interested in heritage and environmental issues. Details of how to join can be found in your local library.

Save Britain's Heritage
3 Park Square West, London NW1 4LJ.
From its beginnings in 1975, SAVE has placed special emphasis on the possibilities of alternative use for historic buildings. If there is a particular building which you are concerned about saving, send a photograph of it and information to the address above.

The Victorian Society
1 Priory Gardens, London W4 1TT.
The society has been campaigning to preserve architecture of the nineteenth and early twentieth century since 1956. Under the Town & Country Planning Acts, the society is consulted on all listed building applications involving demolition.

Historical Association
59a Kennington Park Road, London SE11 4JH.
Eighty branches of the society throughout the country try to develop public interest in all aspects of history, including local and contemporary history.

Society for the Protection of Ancient Buildings
37 Spital Square, London E1 6DY.
Founded in 1877 by William Morris, SPAB was the first body to concern itself with the repair and protection of Britain's architectural heritage. Today the society plays an important role as a leading expert on aspects of the maintenance and preservation of old buildings.

British Association for Local History
43 Bedford Square, London WC1B 3DP.
Previously the Standing Conference on Local History, the new association has more than one thousand members, consisting of individuals and local history organizations.

6

THE POWER AND THE GLORY

Since the 1960s there has been considerable ill feeling directed towards the planners and opportunist developers who planted bleak tower blocks, and ploughed urban motorways through our Victorian suburbs in the name of progress. Thankfully we now seem to have a greater sense of the past. The efforts of dedicated conservation groups and determined individuals have made us more aware of the shocking rate at which history has been disappearing with each swing of the ball and chain. In the twenty years since that decade of national vandalism and high-rise

madness, we have begun to recognize our heritage, and have made greater efforts to save it. But how old is historic – and what is it that makes a building worth saving?

No one would dream of demolishing Buckingham Palace, or the Houses of Parliament, yet we nearly lost one of the country's best-known buildings. Very few people in fact even knew that it was under threat, perhaps because it seems too young to be historic. . . Battersea Power Station, dominating London's waterfront, is as much part of our national

Battersea Power Station – flagship of the 1930s.

Manchester Town Hall – one of the fine examples of our inter-war heritage which lifted the spirit of industrial cities during the Depression.

heritage as Westminster Abbey or the Tower of London. It was built in one of our greatest periods of architectural confidence and optimism. But despite its functional grandeur and importance, its future was in the balance. Fortunately – and quite rightly – Battersea Power Station, designed by Sir Giles Gilbert Scott, is now a Grade I listed building.

When the switches were first thrown in 1933, and the 100,000 hp turbos hummed into life on their throne-like dais, it was hailed as a miracle of modern times. They called it the Palace of Power, with its brown-brick fluted chimneys soaring as high as St Paul's. The interior was breathtaking – shafts of sunlight streamed through tall windows into the pillared turbine hall, 145 m (475 ft) long and 44 m (199 ft) high. The walls were faced with blue-grey terracotta, and powerful machinery gleamed like a vision of the future. High in the roof, where boiler-suited technicians of this brave new world strode confidently with clip-boards, the control room walls were lined with marble. Parquet floors and brass hand rails gleamed in concealed lighting beneath a glass ceiling.

There had been some concern about building an obtrusive power station in a residential area in the heart of London. Questions were even raised in the House about the damage sulphur fumes might cause to pictures in the National Gallery. But a quarter of a million pounds worth of advanced technology, using gas 'scrubbers' and eliminators, ensured that only whisps of harmless water vapour drifted from the chimneys. So efficient was Battersea that surplus heat was funnelled beneath the Thames to a housing estate on the opposite bank.

'We have done our utmost to prevent the station being a blot on the landscape,' said Sir Francis Fladgate, chairman of the London Power Company. 'We believe we have a building which, in beauty and symmetry of design, both within and without, is of its class second to none in the world. We have built a power station which is both ornamental and architecturally dignified.'

Battersea was a triumph of design which almost vanished in our less appreciative age. When it closed, it fell victim to a Central Electricity Generating Board policy of not maintaining obsolete power stations.

The meeting of art and industry – Wallis, Gilbert & Partners' Hoover Factory at Perivale.

Its fate seemed almost sealed when, in 1978, the Department of the Environment declined to list it as an historically important building. The plight of the decaying shell came to the attention of members of the Thirties Society who are dedicated to preserving our inter-war heritage. They campaigned to save Battersea and, in October 1980, succeeded when the power station was included in a list of fifty buildings of the period considered worthy of protection. The cost of repairing the damage hastened by years of neglect is estimated at six million pounds, but Battersea now has a bright, safe future as a pleasure park. It will stand permanently as a symbol of its age. A cathedral to electricity, the new source of power that meant so much in terms of bringing us into the modern world. Although Battersea is perhaps the best-known, the inter-war years saw the construction of many fine buildings dedicated to industry.

From impressive buildings down to the smallest everyday items such as cigarette cases and cups and saucers, design had been turned upside down. The woodland tendrils of Art Nouveau inspired by the painstaking Arts and Crafts Movement, wilted in the heat of Progress. Mass production and new materials like bakelite and chromium became the rage, fashioned in bold simple lines inspired by the age of ocean liners, aeroplanes and electricity. Style was everything, and ideas were borrowed freely from the sleek lines of machines. In turn, the factories which housed them, producing products for the masses, were turned into temples to technical achievement. The world of industry meant progress and captured the spirit of the times. A tidal wave of low, white factories with long, artistic windows spread along the A40, through estates of geometric, flat-topped homes. Art and industry went hand in hand, leading Southern England from the slums to a clean new life in commuterland.

Inspired architects, such as Wallis, Gilbert & Partners built the futuristic Hoover factory at Perivale, with windows that curled round corners, squat towers and an entrance as bold as an Aztec temple. Like many other factories and homes of the period it was finished in startling white, harmonizing with the philosophy of the influential designer Le

61

Corbusier: 'Cleanliness shows objects in their absolute veracity,' he preached. 'It implies the obligation of absolute purity.' Wallis Gilbert went on to turn the suburban by-pass into a place of wonder, building streamlined Taj Mahals for India Tyres, Coty, Wrigley and Burton's.

Perhaps their greatest achievement was the Firestone Tyre Factory on the old London Airport road, now lost forever despite the valiant efforts of conservation groups. The death knell for the Firestone Building with its classic Art Deco styling, was sounded when the company ceased production in Brentford and sold the building. Both the Thirties Society, and Save Our Heritage contacted the Department of the Environment and pleaded that it should be given urgent spot-listing as a protected building. The local planning authority sent a photographer down to help them consider the case, but events were moving faster than the blinking of an eye. Demolition men telephoned the Department of the Environment to ask if the spot-listing had been approved. As usual the wheels of the Civil Service turned slowly and a decision had not been reached. Soon afterwards, on a Saturday morning in August 1980, the bulldozers moved in and by the end of the weekend before the Department had returned to work in Marsham Street, it had been levelled.

In its own way the Firestone Building was as important as Battersea but it was too late to save. No listed Victorian building can now be demolished without reference to the Victorian Society, who preserve our Victorian heritage. But the 1930s were

A home of your own: Gipton estate outside Leeds was one of the biggest built in the country between the wars.

only fifty years ago and for some reason, we do not think it long enough ago to be interesting or important.

'The 1930s Society aims to ensure the preservation of the best buildings from the 1914 to 1939 period,' says spokesman Gavin Stamp. 'Architecture of that time is often nearing a dangerous age. Redevelopment is proceeding faster than public awareness. Far too few buildings of the inter-war period have been given statutory protection.

The wanton demolition of the Firestone Building on the Great West Road showed that even buildings of immense public appeal are not exempt from the demolition squad's ball-and-chain. Other master-pieces – whether Art Deco, or International Style, neo-Tudor or neo-Georgian – are still potential-ly at risk. The Thirties Society exists to campaign for them.'

As Orwell drafted his *Road to Wigan Pier* and marchers tramped in blankets from Jarrow, the traditional centres of heavy industry in the North of England bore the weight of the Great Depression. The South, meanwhile was enjoying an unprece-dented economic boom. In the same way that elec-tronics are the growth area of the 1980s, light indus-try was the salvation of the 1930s, epitomized by the electrical industry with all its new gadgets and appliances.

Along with increased manufacturing and the age of the motor car came the growth of our suburbs. A new era of city-dwelling had dawned and in London the Piccadilly Line snaked out to residential areas where country met town. Stations, such as Osterley and Piccadilly Circus, recently listed as protected buildings, featured passageways and decorative tiles which reflected the mood of the period.

Home for millions meant a modern box-shaped house on ambitious estates – Park Royal, London, and Gipton outside Leeds which was one of the largest residential areas to be built in the 1930s, emphasized the move towards healthy living. 'Beauty as an offspring of science' was the theme of suburban house design. 'Fresh air to breathe, sunshine, cleaner food and cleaner houses; to say nothing of the joys of days in the open on the tennis courts and golf courses, which are within easy distance of many of the estates. . . .' as one sales brochure bubbled. The great house-building boom between the wars, when four

Splendour in the suburbs: The Regal Super Cinema, Leeds, opened in 1936 after being built in just 27 weeks. It boasted 1500 seats and the biggest theatre car-park in Britain. House Full notices went up on opening night for Eddie Cantor and Ethel Merman in 'Stripe Me Pink'. In 1964 the Regal closed after screening 'The Longest Day'. It was considered a prime site for redevelopment and was demolished to make way for the clang, clang, clang of supermarket trollies.

A Super Cinema for the Suburbs.

THE STALLS FOYER

A Few Facts Concerning the REGAL CINEMA. ::

THE OPENING of the Regal Cinema marks the first stage in the development of a stupendous scheme for providing the highest class Cinema Entertainment for those residents of the Suburbs of Leeds who, hitherto, have had few opportunities of enjoying the masterpieces of film productions under ideal conditions.

In opening the Regal Cinema, the promoters have held steadfast to their original policy ; namely, to give suburban cinema-lovers all the comfort and convenience which has hitherto been associated only with the Super Cinemas in the heart of the City.

November 16th will be a date to remember long after the Regal Cinema has become an institution of the district. It opens a new era of entertainment in the City of Leeds, and denotes a spirit of enterprise that puts the bogey of depression to flight.

million homes were built, was spurred by the arrival of building societies. The mortgage was born – and for £645, or 17/10d a week, a young couple could buy a semi in Bexley Heath, 'just twenty-nine minutes from London Bridge.' They curved in rows, flat-topped and white, with neatly-trimmed gardens and metal window frames to let in light and air. The dream of Dunroamin and Journey's End, with sunbathing and robust hikes at weekends was paradise itself. The handy station, clean shops and neat houses were the vision of the new city which left even those wary of change in exhuberant mood.

There was a new vitality as suburbia skipped airily from the grim memories of one war and slipped dangerously towards the next. The poor had an opportunity to escape from the slums into more than a million new council houses. The middle classes, praising the miracle of the mortgage could afford a home of their own. For the wealthy, perhaps more than anyone, life was totally different. As demand for houses grew they became smaller and more compact. There was no longer room for vast kitchens below stairs manned by armies of servants. Designers moved the kitchen to the ground floor to save space, and transformed it into a well-lit showcase of electrical appliances. It became fashionable, not only to have a gleaming kitchen, but to be seen in it too. Women had worked while their husbands were away at war, and many now had careers. They were stylish, athletic, independent, and the kitchen – no longer a place of working class drudgery – expressed their newly-found freedom perfectly. Art, science and industry worked in harmony in the modern home.

Interior designers were engaged by the nouveau riche, who wanted the best the age had to offer but lacked the confidence to choose it. As the standard of living increased, and a feeling of optimism grew, the modernism of Continental design spread into Britain. Twenty years later when the post-war world demanded new architecture, it was again to become a symbol of the future.

The 1930s, perhaps above everything was the age of travel. The conquest of the air was as significant as the space missions of the 1960s and 1970s. It was appropriate that as science and technology became harnessed for the masses, the world also became accessible – for those who could afford it. Travel was suddenly fashionable and stylish. Ocean liners became floating palaces, fitted out by the finest

ABOVE: *The Pier Head, Liverpool, where the great liners once docked. The influence of the sea helped the city to rebuild and survive the Depression of the 1930s.*
BELOW: *The* Daily Express *building, Manchester, built between the wars and reminiscent of the flying bridge of an ocean liner.*

interior designers of the day. Shipping lines vied with each other to create the most opulent accommodation. The French liner *Normandie*, launched in 1935 set the standard featuring a 107 m (350 ft) dining room, with huge chandeliers and walls of glass made in the workshops of Rene Lalique.

The sleek, uncluttered line of the great ships extended its influence, curiously, in airport design.

Liverpool, for instance, which surprisingly survived the worst of the 1930s depression, celebrated the period with a wealth of fine architecture. The new Liverpool Airport was a homage to the wonders of flight – twin hangars were decorated with colossal outstretched wings and even drainpipes had aviation motifs. In shape and style it was strongly reminiscent of the great Cunarders which sailed into the port.

'The only way to cross . . .' the ocean liner summed up the spirit and style of the age.

TOP: *Liverpool's Forum Cinema, a classic of 1930s architecture inspired by the form of the ocean liner.* BOTTOM: *Liverpool Airport, a celebration of the conquest of the air, curiously took its inspiration from the sleek lines of luxury Cunarders.*

The Adelphi Hotel, Liverpool, refurbished between the wars to match the style and elegance of the Cunard passengers who stayed there.

The Mersey Tunnel: one of the highpoints of Liverpool's inter-war years heritage, and a triumph of engineering.

It used to be said that a liner was 'the only way to cross', and when a luxurious voyage was complete, passengers expected to stay in an hotel of equal grandeur. Liverpool's answer was the *Adelphi*, built in late Edwardian days and sumptuously refurbished between the wars. Hotels, like department stores and factories were a focus for the rich talents of architects and designers. Liverpool emerged from the slump with a dazzling array of buildings, from the Mersey Tunnel with its geometric ventilation shafts, to the bold, confident lines of Barclay's Bank dedicated to the power of commerce.

There is one building however which will outlive them all – the rose pink sandstone splendour of St James' Cathedral – the largest Anglican cathedral in the world. It was said to be John Betjeman's favourite building, and it would be a rare man indeed who is not moved by its scale and magnificence. Sir Giles Gilbert Scott who built Battersea's cathedral of electricity, was the architect of this cathedral to God perched high above the Mersey. His father planned the Albert Memorial and restored many of our great cathedrals, including Hereford, Lichfield, Ripon and Salisbury, in addition to founding the Society for the Protection of Ancient Buildings. In 1934 Sir Giles received a gold medal from the Royal Society of Arts as 'the builder of a lasting heritage for Britain'. He began his career articled to church architect Temple

Moore. When the competition to design Liverpool's Anglican cathedral was announced, Moore was so busy with pages of designs he was barely aware that his young apprentice was constantly late for work. Whenever the master architect noticed, he would scribble disapproving notes on Scott's drawing board, ordering him to be punctual. Little did he realize that his pupil had been toiling late into the night with an eye on the same competition. Scott's inspired designs impressed the judging committee, and he won outright. Work began on the cathedral, which has been praised for its simplicity and serenity, in

The stylishness of the 1930s shown in this Mersey Tunnel ventilation shaft sums up the confidence of 1930s design.

the mid 1930s. More than forty years later it was completed to stand as the city's most important contribution to the age.

We tend to think of the past in terms of monarchs – the Elizabethen age, the Victorian age, the Edwardians – but there are other ways of defining the great eras of history, and Britain between the wars was certainly one. Just how long it remains with us depends upon our vigilance, and the efforts of caring people like the Thirties Society. As for Sir Giles Gilbert Scott, his achievements have become part of the fabric of English life. One of his best known memorials is with us still, though slowly disappearing – the familiar red telephone box. . .

FIND OUT FOR YOURSELF

The Thirties Society
3 Park Square West
London NW1
The heritage of the inter-war years is perhaps at more risk of disappearing than that of any other period. Often force of numbers is the only effective argument against official intransigence. The Thirties Society is badly in need of more members and welcomes enquiries.

Liverpool Cathedral, Giles Gilbert Scott's architectural triumph overlooking the Mersey.

7

FAMILY ALBUMS

Click! Every time you take a photograph, you create a piece of history. A very small piece, admittedly, and only a few seconds old, but history is a continuous process and given time, that fading sepia portrait of great grandmother, or a dog-eared snap of a pre-war camping holiday could prove to be as valuable an historical source as registers, archives and ledgers.

A snapshot album, or a box of family photographs is more than just memories – an average collection can take us back three or four generations and in

The family snapshot as a valuable historical record: there were some everyday activities few people thought to record. Years later they provide a fond reminder of the way we were.

some cases, to the early days of popular photography at the turn of the century.

Victorians were fond of photographing their buildings. Then-and-now pictures make interesting comparisons as many of the original buildings and places photographed then still survive today. But while the great city builders were recording their

achievements, the ordinary man was charting his own progress. In the early days of photography from about 1860 onwards, anyone who wanted his likeness taking needed money and patience. The ordeal of the Victorian portrait studio began with the fitting of an iron clamp to keep the sitter's head from moving. It rose from a heavy metal base on the floor and

BELOW: *Photographs of people at work – as in the case of this Edwardian printer – were also popular subjects with studio photographers.*

RIGHT: *The neck clamp on this young gentleman appears to be so tight that he is clutching the back of the chair for support. The base is just visible behind his polished boots.*

T. BARKER.   R. COPELAND.

ABOVE: *A man with his moleskin breeks cuts a commanding figure. Note the base of the metal stand which clamped him firmly in position.*

LEFT: *When work was over the play began – families saved to have their sporting achievements captured for posterity in the studio.*

secured the back of the neck uncomfortably for the half minute exposure time. Even a fixed smile was impossible to hold for so long, which was why the vast majority of early sitters looked extremely solemn. The photographer had to check that the framing and focussing were correct, put in a holder for the plate, and then cover up the lens. For the great moment the plate was uncovered and the lens cap removed.

Studios were thoroughly equipped with up to a dozen different backgrounds, from castles and mountains to river scenes. Props and paraphernalia, such as rustic fences, artificial rocks and pieces of furniture were used to liven up the picture, and give the impression of grandeur and magnificence.

Next time you come across an upright, unsmiling figure gazing from an imposing sepia landscape, look at the feet – the heavy cast-iron stand at the neck-clamp can occasionally be seen sticking out behind them.

But even as the portait studios flourished, a revolution was taking place. In 1888 George Eastman patented the first Kodak box camera, and the family snapshot was born. Photography, overnight, became simple. It became increasingly common to find delightfully informal pictures of families and friends and together with studio portraits, there were soon few households without their own photographic collection.

In one place, at least, the family photo collection is being given the recognition it deserves. Manchester Studies is a team of researchers based at Manchester Polytechnic who are interested in the history of the area, and particularly the story of working people and routines of everyday life. At first they found that there were few documents in libraries and record

ABOVE: *The first pair of long trousers – always a milestone in a young man's life. Presumably the boater gave him the air of a man-about-town.*

OPPOSITE BOTTOM: *When the photographer left his studio and took to the streets in search of subjects, families would club together and share the cost of a picture.*

BELOW: *The arrival of the camera made families want to record their progress through life – whether it was used to capture the splendour of a wedding, show the generations living under one roof, or simply to snap some holiday fun.*

The Magic Box

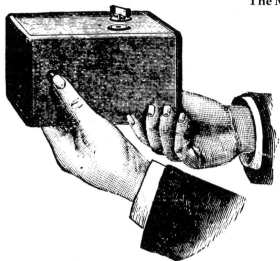

sealed, was sent through the post to the manufacturer for processing. It was returned, in a brown paper parcel with a new film fitted. In many ways they were the forerunner of modern cassette film. 'You press the button – we do the rest,' was the confident slogan. But, at five guineas a time, it was still a rich man's pastime. Keen amateurs included members of the Royal family, who used the de luxe version covered in purple leather, with silver fittings.

By 1900 the box Brownie had appeared on the mass market at the more reasonable price of five shillings. It was still a quarter of a week's wages, but suddenly picture-taking was within reach of even the poorest family. For an extra five pence you could even have the luxury of a viewfinder on top of the camera. Whole generations of box cameras followed.

Folding cameras, which collapsed into a flat, but rather fat box, came on the scene in 1910, and were popular with troops departing for Europe in World War One. Many smuggled them to the front line, where they captured their experiences for the family back home.

The first hand-held cameras opened up a new world for ordinary people. The breakthrough was made by Kodak who introduced film instead of a glass plate. One little black box took a hundred exposures. All the proud owner had to do was point the camera and press the button. Then the whole camera, still

offices that recorded the day-to-day activities of ordinary people, so they set about rescuing and preserving the primary sources of local history. Since 1975 a collection of more than 35,000 photographs has been assembled – the life and times of the people of Manchester through their own reminiscences and pictures. Each faded snapshot receives the same thorough scrutiny and interest as it helps to build a growing picture of their jobs, hobbies, weddings, holidays, clothes, shops, and even their moods.

LEFT: *Smile please! Whenever a photographer appeared everyone wanted to be in on the picture.*

Manchester Studies is the only collection which systematically gathers and stores family photographs. It is open to the public, and copies are sent for displays in local libraries. Great interest has been shown, not only by the public, but by sociologists, local historians and the increasing number of people interested in the history of photography. Television companies too, are among the steady flow of visitors. The designer of a drama production may, for instance, want to know what a school in Wigan looked like in the 1920s, how the teacher and pupils dressed, and all the tiny details of classroom life. By encouraging access to the archive, Manchester Studies

BELOW: *Cycling was the perfect way to escape from the grime of the mill towns at the weekend. The rattle of the local wheelers setting off down cobbled streets was once a familiar sound.*

group keep in close contact with the people who are their main source of supply. Public exhibitions are another way of attracting the interest of possible donors. Audrey Linkman who organizes them, says: 'At small, local exhibitions people came along because they recognize the places, and they want to see if they are on the photographs themselves. We try to get them to go one step further and see themselves as important in history. Without their photographs and documents, historians would have little raw material to work from.'

A direct appeal to the public often generates a response, and Audrey and her colleagues spend time out and about, talking to people in the area. Women's institutes, village clubs and urban community centres are shown slides from the collection – stiff family portraits, little boys proudly posing in their first long trousers, informal snaps taken in back-yards and kitchens. Many have gone home after illustrated talks to rummage through their old photographs again, and see them in a different light. 'They have often lived through the things we are talking about, and will fill us in,' she says. 'It doesn't matter how often I've seen a slide, I can show it for the fifty-eighth time and someone has a new piece of information to offer.'

When business in the studio was slow, early photographers would take their cameras into the streets. Instead of straightfaced children in their Sunday best, they captured charming moments from everyday life. And if parents could not afford an individual snap, they would collect all the children in the street and share the cost. Many of these treasures from the past are still the pride of family collections.

After a slide show the team takes the names and addresses of the audience and visits them in their homes. There they sit down and patiently go through every photograph, asking who it was, when it was taken, and why. The rewarding detail, and the combination of picture and anecdote enables the group to compile well-documented and accurate records of life in the North West. One of their favourites among the 35,000 pictures is an old black and white photograph of a mother washing her children in a tin bath. It plugged an important gap in the day to day activities of life in local terraced

'Didn't we have a lovely time . . .' seaside photographers made a lucrative living from families on holiday.

THE KODAK.

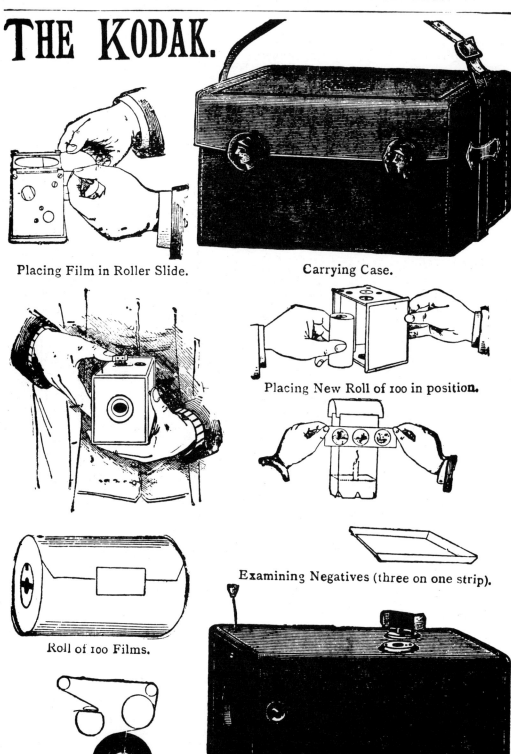

Placing Film in Roller Slide.

Carrying Case.

Placing New Roll of 100 in position.

Examining Negatives (three on one strip).

Roll of 100 Films.

Position of Film in Roller Slide.

Complete Kodak.

homes. Bath night was a regular event, the highlight of the week, but this was one of the few occasions that anyone had thought to record it. Toddlers on the donkeys at Blackpool beach . . . black-edged studies of relatives lost in pit accidents . . . the happy rub shoulders with the sad. After talking to the Manchester Studies team many families have taken a renewed interest in their albums and shoeboxes of pictures, and set about recording life today for future generations.

Manchester Studies group also pursues the moving equivalent of the stills collection. Amateur crime films are, of course, much rarer than snapshots but they still turn up, sometimes from surprisingly rich sources. The North West Film Archive has 400 titles, and as many again awaiting acquisition. They range from people at work, and coach outings to the seaside, to local visits by Royalty and how they celebrated Armistice Day. Some of these films were made by enterprising cinemas which organized annual trips for children who attended the Saturday matinee. They were issued with an attendance card which was stamped each week. If they collected the right number of stamps they qualified for a free day out. One Cheshire cinema took 1,000 children out to a farm in 1909, supervised by only eight adults! They eagerly lined up on the platform of Altrincham station, each faithfully labelled, waiting excitedly for the arrival of the excursion train. The occasion was professionally filmed and then shrewdly shown a few weeks later to enthusiastic parents who paid to see their children on the big screen. In 1937 it was featured again – this time for their own children, to show how mum and dad used to enjoy themselves.

In the collection there are also old promotional and advertising films, made in an attempt to recapture European business for local cotton industries. Most are hand-cranked, showing mill girls in shawls and loom workers operating machinery in their bare feet in case their wooden clogs slipped on the greasy floors. Preserving the film, like all early cine efforts, is a formidable problem. Chemical decomposition has destroyed almost ninety per cent of some original material. Film archive technicians transfer everything they can salvage to modern film to preserve these priceless moments from our past. Jerky memories of wakes weeks, weddings and families larking in the garden are all faithfully copied and stored for future historians.

FACING PAGE: *The Kodak camera was the wonder of the age, bringing photography suddenly within the reach of even the poorest families.*

Rediscovering Family Photographs

'. . . This is my father's brother Bill. He was quite a character. He ran off to join the circus at one time, then he joined the regular army. Finally he settled down and became a miner. When I was small he used to tell me that he dug for black diamonds. I didn't know what they were at the time. . . .'

'. . . We took part in a Sunday school pantomime when we were younger. There's my sister and I in *Babes In The Wood*. I found out recently that this other girl here has the same great grandfather as I do. She was the principal boy . . .'

'. . . Here's my aunt Jane. She was a medium and a very interesting woman. Shortly before my grandfather's death she came to my grandmother and said: "One of us is going to lose a husband." Soon afterwards there was the pit accident, and my grandfather died. She used to stop people in the street and tell them things quite out of the blue . . .'

'. . . Now this is my grandmother and her sister Ethel – you notice Ethel's wearing a high-necked blouse. When she was sixteen there was trouble at home one evening. Her father had been drinking. Ethel was rather cheeky to him, and he thought she was impudent. He picked up a knife from the table and threw it at her. It stuck in the back of her neck and made a wound about half an inch long and half an inch deep. The policeman was called, and eventually he was sent to the Quarter Sessions to be tried. Ethel's bloodstained blouse was produced as evidence and held up in court. He was given two months hard labour. Ethel always wore a blouse with a high neck to hide the scar after that . . .'

FIND OUT FOR YOURSELF

When we look at family pictures for historical information, there are particular questions to ask: Who were the people photographed? Who took the photograph? Where was it taken, and in what year? What story is there behind it?

It is important to keep this information in a well-organized record, because as it becomes more complete a good family and social history begins to build. Do not write in ball-point pen on the photographs, as the writing may show on the front – it is much better to keep notes in a notebook, or a loose-leaf file. Keep a note, too, of details of fashion, relationships, domestic items in the pictures, and town or landscapes.

It is not unusual in a collection of photographs to find one or two that date from the end of the last century. They may well be brown in colour, or hand-tinted, and be very formal portraits. Quite often they are very good in quality, and offer a fascinating insight into the past.

Look carefully to see: If they are studio portraits using painted backcloths. What studio props are used – aspidistras were very common. If there is evidence of a clamp to keep the person sitting still. What dress people felt it was appropriate to wear.

Photography is not only looking at snapshots, it can also be the study or collection of cameras themselves. Early wooden cameras are not easy to find and are expensive. Old box cameras, folding pocket cameras, or post-war plastic cameras can still be found in second-hand shops and are an interesting starting-point for a collection.

Manchester Studies
Manchester Polytechnic
Cavendish House
Cavendish Street
Manchester M15 6BG.

Archives of photographs, films and oral history recordings on the lives of working people.

Kodak Museum
Wealdstone
Harrow HA1 4TY
Middlesex.

All aspects of the history of photography, with displays of objects and artefacts, as well as an exhibition which is changed every few months.

National Museum of Photography, Film & Television
Prince's View
Bradford BD5 0AE
West Yorkshire.

A new museum concerned with the past, present and future of the moving image, and technology involved.

Victoria and Albert Museum
London SW7 2RL.

In addition to occasional photographic exhibitions, the museum has more than 300,000 photographs in its collection and is well worth a visit.

8

FORTRESS BRITAIN

No matter where you travel in Britain there is evidence everywhere of our military past, from Iron Age hill forts, to Roman walls and World War II concrete pill-boxes. The remnants of Britain's fighting history, scattered around our coast and towns, stretch back more than 2,000 years and strangely, most of them are not offensive, but defensive. The reason is not only because we are an island race but because we are a rather belligerent one. Long before the days when Britain ruled the waves and carved the greatest empire man has ever known, we have been constantly at war with our neighbours. And, in a climate of invasion and threat of invasion, the coastline became encircled with a mantle of military defences.

These were constructed around our vital ports from earth, stone and steel in massive feats of engineering as our naval heritage grew. In the days of sail the navy had to station itself according to whom we were fighting – and the prevailing winds. When Britain took up arms against Spain, Plymouth came to the fore; against the Dutch it was Chatham on the Medway. When the enemy was France, as it constantly seemed to be, Portsmouth was the home of the British fleet. Perhaps more than any other town, it has retained the complete story of our coastal defences. Within a few square miles evidence of our military history in architecture and engineering is preserved as a memorial – and a lasting warning – to invaders.

Fortress Britain: Portsmouth's town defences with the Square Tower with its saluting platform and ten-gun battery in the foreground. In the distance an 18-gun emplacement deterred invasion on the seaward side.

Portsmouth owes much of its strategic importance to the thrust of geology – the imperceptible movement of the Downs, the abrasive gouging of rivers and the constant pounding of the sea. Together they forged a natural deep water harbour, protected from the elements by the long, low outline of the Isle of Wight. Around this secure mooring, with its easily-defended mouth, grew facilities to build and maintain a fleet for centuries to come. Alfred sailed from here to fight the Danes in AD 897 and one thousand years later, Prince Andrew sailed for the Falklands on the *Invincible*.

Despite the navy's rich and important history, its main role was more often than not, simply to transport the army around. As even the most powerful ship is vulnerable at anchor, Portsmouth developed above all into a great garrison town. Across the bay from present-day Portsmouth stands Porchester Castle, built by the Romans who saw it as the ideal point for a base to defend the estuary. It is situated on an arm of land which curves protectively across the sheltered harbour mouth and its safe anchorage. Roman engineers laid out their castle in a perfect square on the tip of the promontory, with gates in the centre of each wall. As an additional precaution it was equipped with twenty bastions to give legionaries an all-round view, and surrounded by a deep ditch. Porchester formed part of what was known as the Saxon Shore defences – a strategic chain of castles winding along Britain's south coast, from the Wash to Southampton Water.

An early invasion attempt in AD 286, had spurred the Romans to build Porchester Castle. A Saxon fleet was sighted rounding the Isle of Wight, and the Roman galleys immediately put to sea to repel it. Before the battle even had chance to get under way, one of the now-famous Portsmouth fogs suddenly descended and the invaders lost their bearings and were never seen again.

King Alfred was the first British monarch to realize the importance of stepping-up naval and garrison defences at Portsmouth. In AD 897 he began building ships, and soon had a fleet competent enough to take on a sizeable band of marauding Vikings. When the warning cry went up, the Danes must have been a formidable sight, moving menacingly in battle formation up Spithead, with a square sail amidships and twenty oars each side. Alfred's ships, sturdily built from local Hampshire oak, met them with a volley of arrows, before drifting broadside and engaging the Vikings in hand-to-hand fighting. To a beleagured island race, Alfred's victory created new confidence both in the navy and the strength of Portsmouth's defences. King Harold later sailed up the Channel in the same way to counter the Norman invasion in 1066 only to arrive too late to prevent the enemy landing in Pevensey Marshes. When he caught up with them on land, the resulting encounter was the Battle of Hastings.

Nature was soon to intervene again in the shaping of Portsmouth's defences. The top end of the harbour began to silt up by the end of the Norman period, diminishing Porchester Castle's strategic importance. Shipping moved to seek fresh shelter at nearby Portsea, a natural deep water harbour which was to become a place of great importance in British history. The first big fleet left Portsmouth in 1194 when Richard I led a hundred ships out to the Crusades, pausing en route to settle a small difference in France.

Piece by piece Portsmouth's coastline expanded into an almost continuous fortress in an attempt to repel attacks on the Fleet. Southsea Castle juts seaward to the right, protecting the town behind it. Fort Monckton, on the coast in the foreground, defended the other flank of the estuary.

Outside London, no other city was more frequently visited by Royalty who recognized the value of its defences. But as it became widely known across the Channel that Portsmouth had become the post of kings, the town became a prime target for attack. Breaching its already solid fortifications would have constituted a great propaganda victory, as well as seizing command of the waterway between Britain and France.

A few successes were scored before Portsmouth began to seriously consolidate its defences – pirates almost burned the place down in 1266; and in 1357 a raiding party from the French navy ransacked the town and massacred much of the population. They returned on three more occasions in the next ten years, until Britain gathered together a fleet large enough to cross the Channel and retaliate. The result was an uneasy peace during which Portsmouth built with determination to ensure that it would never be humiliated again.

A Round Tower was constructed overlooking Spithead and the port, with cannon equipped to fire seawards across the harbour and over the next few hundred years a range of ramparts, known as the Long Curtain, was developed to strengthen the defence of the approaches. Piece by piece the gaps were plugged and the fortifications grew. Henry VII built a Square Tower, facing out to sea, which was so well constructed that centuries later it was still being used as a powder magazine. As an indication of the growing links between Royalty and Portsmouth, Henry also provided the money for a gun platform to be connected to the Square Tower, for ten-gun salutes to hail the return of his fleet. The massive job of strengthening the defences meant that no new warships were laid in his reign but – anxious to maintain his ships in fighting trim – the first dry dock in Britain was built there in 1495.

Portsmouth began to take on the air of a town under siege, with bastions, ramparts and moats almost constantly under construction. A cornerstone of the system was Southsea Castle, built in 1544 to command the vital deep water channel which passed close to the shore. By this time artillery was emerging

Southsea Castle, built in 1544, commanded the deep water channel which ran close to the shore. It was from here that Henry watched the Mary Rose go down. Many alterations were made over the years to improve its defences. By the nineteenth century it was almost lost in a vast system of granite fortifications stretching along the coast.

The Round Tower and the Square Tower marked Portsmouth's growing importance as a garrison town and home of the fleet. Their purpose was to guard the narrow harbour mouth and protect the Royal dockyard.

as an effective weapon of defence and Southsea, squat with immensely thick walls, was specifically designed for maximum firepower. The square keep had gun platforms overlooking more rows of heavy artillery on the walls below. Henry VIII took a personal interest in its design, the castle's reassuring appearance on the Portsmouth skyline proved to be timely. Less than a year after the completion of Southsea, a signal arrived that a huge fleet of two hundred French ships was heading for Portsmouth under full sail. As a great naval battle, the ensuing conflict was something of a damp squib. Though the weather looked unsettled, there was barely more than a light breeze, and neither fleet could manoeuvre into a position of advantage, although several English ships drifting listlessly within sight of Southsea Castle were captured by the French in an exchange of fire. The king was pacing the ramparts when the unpredictable Channel weather turned into a sudden squall, catching the 500 ton *Mary Rose* broadside. All her portholes, just sixteen inches from the waterline, were wide open for action and she quickly filled up and sank without trace. Three centuries later Prince Charles, in diving gear, felt his way along the hull of the *Mary Rose*, lying in the silt, and unexpectedly encountered the remains of one of its crewmen.

The skirmish with the French underlined the importance of Portsmouth's defences, and successive monarchs added to Henry VIIIs artillery fortifications. Taxes were used to pay for defence building and dockyard maintenance. Elizabeth I, who launched and encouraged the great age of seafaring, enthusiastically promoted a public lottery – thought to be the first in Britain. Tickets, at ten shillings a time, raised money for a new square tower at Sally Port – the breach in the walls through which defenders could 'sally forth'.

The need for defence increased as the nature of weaponry changed. The reliability and effectiveness of artillery was moving ahead steadily, and new styles of fortification began to reflect its importance. Behind the naval flag-flying, the army began to play a key role in Portsmouth's defence.

With the Restoration, Charles II, worried about Holland's naval power, shrewdly hired the services of a Dutchman, Bernard de Gomme, to modify Portsmouth's defence system. For twenty years from 1665 fortifications around the town were reshaped, and the old ramparts drastically remodelled. De Gomme, a military engineer who had served with the Royalists in the Civil War, turned Portsmouth into a formidable fortress – fitting the gates with artillery platforms and constructing a round, eighteen-gun battery facing seawards, to provide flanking fire along the city walls. Access to the beach to repel an invasion landing was through a unique sally port, designed with an S-bend so that assault parties could not rush the defences. A small gun-turret overlooked it as an additional precaution.

A hundred shipwrights were employed in the naval dockyard. By Victorian times, as a measure of Portsmouth's importance the workforce had increased to 6,000, with an annual wage bill of a third of a million pounds. The huge defence expansion was precipitated by yet another threat from France in the shape of an attempted Napoleonic invasion.

For centuries the bustle of war preparations was a familiar sight and sound in the harbourside inns of Portsmouth. They rang with the songs of sailors embarking for action while soldiers marched outside changing guard along the fortifications.

One thatched pub, the Waggon and Lamb, served ale to Tudor ratings setting off to engage the French. Later, with its name changed to the George, the hostelry provided bed and breakfast for Nelson before he sailed to take on the same old adversary in 1803. Senior officers patronized the Star and Garter, along the road, within earshot of the ribald clamour of drunken midshipmen in the Blue Posts coaching house.

The shadow of Napoleon brought about the apex of artillery defence – the star fort, of which only two survive in Britain. Fort Cumberland, the last bastioned fort built in Britain, with its low-profile five-pointed spread, can only be effectively seen from the air. It guarded Langstone Harbour, alongside Portsmouth town, with emplacements for eighty-one guns manned by the Royal Marine Artillery. Although fewer cannons were needed as weaponry it became most accurate and efficient.

Like de Gomme's defences, and many others along Britain's coastline, Fort Cumberland was built with convict labour. The enormous amount of stone and brick devoured by the star fort made it backbreaking work, and the enforced labourers from prison hulks moored in the harbour staged frequent rebellions and escape attempts. Porchester Castle, disease-ridden and overcrowded housed 8,000 more, from a variety of countries. Most were French, some were American as Britain was also at war with the United States, while others had been taken from ships of many nationalities which had traded with our enemies. Some prisoners even tried to tunnel out and escape by sea, but in a town with Portsmouth's watchful defences, there was little chance of getting far.

The exile of Napoleon did little to lessen the ever-present possibility of French invasion. His nephew Napoleon III revived old fears, leading Palmerston to order a whole ring of forts – five in the Solent and six along the ridge of chalk downs overlooking the town. Although never used in action, they were virtually impregnable, and a masterpiece of military design. Many people however, called them Palmerston's Follies, because their guns pointed inland, away from the direction of attack by sea. Military experts were in fact worried about the possibility of an encircling French attack from behind.

It was one of the most extravagant and expensive fort-building programmes in history, turning Portsmouth into the world's most heavily-defended naval base. The heavy guns facing inland were protected with bomb-proof casements. In case they were over-run, their blind side was covered by long, heavily armed fortifications called the Hilsea Lines. Massive earthworks were built at Southsea Castle, which bristled with artillery. An outer ring of steel and granite forts, with revolving gun turrets, emerged from the estuary to provide a first line of defence. The cost was rumoured to be half the national income, but by the time the ring of firepower was constructed, the threat of invasion had receded and advances in defence technology had made the artillery used quite obsolete.

Portsmouth's earthworks, sunken forts and Victorian granite fortifications were used in World War II as cover for the departing D-Day army. The landings were planned in Portsmouth, and the whole town was turned into a vast military base. Palmerston's Follies were used as a base for anti-aircraft positions – but the world of warfare had changed beyond recognition. For the first time in almost 2,000 years, the castles and fortifications were defenceless against the unforeseen threat of the aeroplane . . .

OPPOSITE TOP: *Portsmouth was an ideal naval base, but its vulnerable estuary came under constant threat from seaward attack. The harbour mouth is heavily guarded by an array of fortifications which grew over the centuries.* OPPOSITE BOTTOM: *The Mary Rose emerging from the sea to be seen again for the first time in centuries. At the moment this picture was taken a bolt on the cradle sheared, threatening to send the historic wreck to the bottom again.* ABOVE: *Fort Widley, in a commanding position on the Downs above Portsmouth, was built in response to the Royal Commission of 1860. The low-profile artillery fort was intended to counter attempts to destroy the dockyard below by bombardment.*

FIND OUT FOR YOURSELF

Portsmouth City Museum
Museum Road
Old Portsmouth PO1 2LJ.

In Portsmouth the whole story of Britain's defences is telescoped into one town – but take a walk in your own area and look for evidence of how, over the centuries, we have attempted to resist invasion. Many rural railway lines and colliery approaches still have evidence of concrete tank traps and pill boxes from World War II. Our towns have the remains of Roman walls and medieval gateways, and where they have long since vanished, some are still commemorated in the names of streets.

From prehistoric earthworks to moated Tudor houses, Britain has been vigilant against the threat of attack. Your museum may have early maps of local fortifications, and many seaside resorts have the rusting remains of coastal defences from the last war. They provide a unique glimpse of a piece of our history which, in the age of the nuclear weapon, may never been seen again.

9

DIRTY OLD TOWN

Twice a week sixteen million viewers tune in to an intimate look at life in an industrial community. Coronation Street, with its terraced houses, corner shop, cosy local and railway viaduct has been a familiar part of the British scene for a quarter of a century. The intrigues and romances are, for many, as fascinating as the lives of those around them.

Coronation Street has the kind of strong community spirit once found in row upon row of identical streets built, literally in their hundreds of thousands, to accommodate the population pouring into cities to work in the new factories and mills. The programme's popularity shows that, perhaps in some way, we treasure this part of our industrial heritage. Every town and city has streets like Coronation Street which are still home to millions of people. They were never ideal – many had inadequate sanitation, plumbing, heating and ventilation. Frequently the amenities were poor, although most street corners had a shop or pub. There was undoubtedly poverty, but it was compensated by a rich community life. The sense of security and belonging, even today, seems to outweigh the drawbacks, especially when the alternative might be a tower block. Many people like living in them, and what is more they are capable of being extended and improved, instead of being bulldozed into vast empty tracts of rubble.

Housing, however, is only symptomatic of the problem of our industrial heritage. Rows of sentry-like terraces grew as a result of industry. It is easy to forget that before the eighteenth century, factories were almost unknown. Britain was solidly based on agriculture and the change, when it came, was so great and so rapid that we call it the Industrial Revolution.

The early image of manufacturing was far removed from what we know today. The cradles of industry, around which wealthy towns sprang up, were often set in idyllic, pastoral landscapes. One of the first, and best preserved factories is Quarry Bank textile

mill at Styal, Cheshire, founded by Ulsterman Samuel Greg in 1784. The iron men who pioneered the Industrial Revolution built wherever was handiest, in Greg's case near a canal. There were no

Coronation Street – millions still yearn for the strong community spirit.

93

Quarry Bank Mill at Styal, one of the rural cradles of the Industrial Revolution.

great cities where labour was freely available: they constructed their factories and set about attracting workers to them. Local people, more used to working to the flow of the seasons, and the pattern of the sun, were at first cautious about a new world governed by the rattle of machines. Good employers looked after their workers, providing them with reasonable, if basic, accommodation. Greg went further, building a school, churches and a shop for his tiny industrial community.

'When Quarry Bank Mill was built in the lovely valley, local people regarded it with anxiety,' says David Sekers, curator of the mill now owned by the National Trust. 'Their resentment and fear were based on the fact that it looked like a workhouse, and spoiled the landscape. Even in those days there were conservationists who cared about what

happened to the land. They feared too for the health of the workforce labouring in such a place, but the mill stayed.

'Although Greg was enlightened, he was governed by self interest. When he built a village, it was so he could keep the best of his workforce. When he built an apprentice house, it was to look after youngsters so that they would work better. When he employed a factory doctor, it was to keep them healthy to work the long hours he demanded.'

In its heyday about one third of Quarry Bank Mill's 500 workers were children. From the moment the mill clock struck at dawn, until it signalled 'clocking off time' at night, they worked flat out, forced to follow the rhythm of the machines. To country

David Sekers, director of Styal Museum. The mill has been lovingly preserved and attracts thousands of visitors each year.

people cotton meant a confinement they hated. Their only consolation was the peace of the valley when work was over. After a hard day at the mill, Styal workers did not face a journey over grimy cobbles, through sooty air, just a pleasant rural walk. However, they were probably too exhausted to appreciate it by then.

The face of industry, however, was soon to change. As the revolution accelerated industry congregated around raw materials and centres of transport. The unfamiliar silhouette of the factory meant work for a growing population and attracted by labour, more manufacturers moved in. Within a short time our industrial cities were born, and expanded at an alarming rate. In the hard reality of nineteenth-century business, the good intentions of Mr Greg were soon forgotten. In the 1820s and 1830s steam power hissed and puffed a promise of great prosperity for mill owners. Instead of locating their mills where there was water, they built them near the biggest pool of labour. Factories sprang up shoulder to shoulder with housing, and health problems arose. Unlike Styal, the terraced houses of the soot-blackened towns had no gardens or sanitation. Up to fifty families shared a single privy, rivers stank appallingly, and conditions in the gloomy mills were unbearably noisy, dirty and often without any ventilation. As the wheels of industry turned, skill and enterprise developed alongside invention. Britain's factory system, despite its faults, was copied throughout the world, and its roots, such as Quarry Bank Mill, are worth preserving.

ABOVE: *As the towns hummed with industry around the clock, transport systems evolved to get the workers to factories on time. An early Gateshead bus.*

RIGHT: *The world of work . . . the Industrial Revolution brought little rest for those who had to earn a living in our towns and cities.*

There is an area of Burnley known as the Weavers' Triangle, the heart of what was once the cotton weaving capital of the world. Unlike Styal, where the mill was powered by water, Burnley was steam-driven. A forest of chimneys soared above factories clustered around the canal which brought in raw material and took out the finished goods. It was dirty and depressing, and there was scant regard for the quality of life. Every factory, home and steam engine belched smoke constantly, until a heavy pall hung permanently over the town. Although the air is cleaner these days, places like Burnley had a distinctive smell, which many still remember. And since the textile industry has now almost disappeared, what little charm these towns once had has turned to decay.

As Burnley became King Cotton, Bradford across the grey Pennines, rocketed from being a quiet market town to the wool capital of the world in just thirty years. Dominating everything was Lister's Mill, a Venetian finger jabbing skyward against a backdrop of round-shouldered hills. It opened in 1873, and employed 6,000 workers at the height of the wool boom, when the city was submerged in a sea of smoking chimneys. Bradford represents, in some ways, the pinnacle of the industrial age, growing from 5,000 people in 1800, to 100,000 by 1851 – a scale of change which has never been seen in our lifetime.

Bradford's philanthropist was Mr Titus Salt, a forceful mill-magnate, who poured his profits into Saltaire, a utopian model village removed from the squalor of the back-to-backs. His lofty ideals imposed the values of clean living on weary mill workers. Saltaire, magnificently preserved, had no pub to encourage hangovers and bad time-keeping, but an imposing institute, flanked by stone lions representing determination, vigilance, war and peace. They were originally destined for Trafalgar Square until Titus shrewdly bought them for £200. Even at work there was little excuse for earthly thoughts since workers clocking-on-and-off had no alternative but to pass a chapel, built outside the main entrance to inspire their drudgery.

Fighting to preserve our past: Ken Powell of Save Britain's Heritage.

Some people believe that the manufacturing towns of the North of England were merely thrown up for a functional purpose and having served their need, should be left to the demolition squads and the whims of developers. Ken Powell, of Save Britain's Heritage, disagrees: 'Bradford is very much a product of the Pennine landscape,' he says. 'It grows from the soil, and is perhaps even the greatest stone-built city that has ever existed. Great runs of terraced houses climb the hillsides, all uniform, all in harmony. Bradford is a place which still inspires great affection among the people who live there.'

Industry created immense wealth for a handful of industrialists. While some, like Titus Salt, poured it into good works, others acquired a passion for a strong sense of civic pride. Every town and city sought to show its affluence through museums, libraries, art galleries and rolling public parks. Inevitably, the most extravagant showpiece was the seat of power: the town hall. Ironically most of their fussy splendour soon became blackened by soot billowing from the factories which had paid for them. Proud architecture, featuring busts of local worthies, created a veneer of respectability which contrasted vividly with the poverty and deprivation of the industrial working class. Morley, for instance, is a small Yorkshire town near Leeds whose town hall reflects the wealth and influence once exercised by local mill owners. Its finely carved wood, mosaic floors, gleaming brass and beautiful stained glass symbolize the epitome of Victorian industrial achievement. Most of the mayors whose portraits hang in profusion on the walls, were industrialists. Morley town hall says much about the history of a community which, because of the great rollercoaster of industry, grew from little. It stands as a monument both to those who built the mills and those who toiled in them. Even the civic coat of arms features a bobbin, a crossed shovel and a pick above the motto: 'Industry Conquers All.'

Sadly, many of the mills and warehouses – the buildings which produced the wealth to finance civic pride in towns like Morley – have either gone, or fallen into disrepair. In Batley, Yorkshire, there was once a whole street lined with magnificent buildings running downhill from the railway station to the bustling town centre. Now decrepit and decaying, they no longer provide the money upon which such textile towns depended. Batley was once a great

Civic pride: the wealth of the Industrial Revolution was poured into buildings like Morley Town Hall, near Leeds.

Ken Powell in a street of Batley warehouses which once reflected the wealth of the shoddy industry.

centre of the shoddy trade, recycling rags and woollens into blankets and overcoats. The industry declined between the wars, and many of the ambitious, Italian-style buildings – a conscious evocation of the Renaissance – now stand empty, or burned down.

'There is still quite a lot which could be done behind the fine façades,' Ken Powell believes. 'With internal reconstruction, houses, offices or new types of industry could go into them. It is all possible, and has happened elsewhere. People in Bradford, for instance, have regretted many things that have happened in the recent past. The most striking and terrible transformation was the tearing down of a large portion of the city centre. A ring road was driven through, banal office blocks built, and great monuments like Exchange Station, the marvellous market hall, and the Mechanics Institute were randomly destroyed.

'As for significant developments, one of the most exciting has been the recent growth of tourism. It sounds quite crazy, and I am sure that twenty-five years ago anyone suggesting the idea would have been regarded as loony.

Long hours and hard work are reflected in the rough hands and careworn faces of these Northern mill girls.

Forging the future – a blacksmith at work in the Industrial Revolution.

'When everyone worked in the mills it was not very interesting. Nowadays very few people do, even in Bradford. We are moving into what is being called the Post Industrial Society, and traditional working methods are becoming fascinating. People come to Bradford to see monuments to Lister and Saltaire, the mills and warehouses – it really is an experience Industrial towns are moving towards an appreciation of their past, with a determination to push forward into a prosperous future.'

A rare break in a Bolton bottling plant to celebrate the Coronation of King George VI.

One problem, of course, is that some buildings are so far gone that it is impossible to preserve them. In Manchester it is not uncommon to see a beautiful Georgian warehouse slowly tumbling into a canal. In London's Camden Lock it would probably be saved . . . why not elsewhere?

Manchester Heritage Park is living proof that with interest and commitment, new life can be breathed into industrial decay. It has always been a city of firsts – the first canal, the Bridgewater, terminates there, and it is also the home of the world's first passenger railway station. In what was originally an American concept, local authorities are now working alongside voluntary groups to save city buildings by creating the country's first heritage park. Manchester's Roman fort is being made into a tourist attraction, Liverpool Road Station, which once saw the first rail passengers, is a science museum, a disused market hall has a space museum inside and the city's Central Station is being restored as a trade centre.

There are, however, communities which have bad memories of their industrial past, and do not care to be associated with it. But some argue that it is

OPPOSITE TOP & ABOVE: *When factories sprang up in the industrial towns, working conditions were often dirty and dangerous. Two apprentices pour molten iron in a foundry. Men work with unguarded blades in a sawmill.*

BOTTOM LEFT: *When coal was king – pit brow lassies on their way to work at a Lancashire pit.*

important to have a yardstick for future generations to see for themselves how progress has been made. Without places like Quarry Bank Mill, which puts money back into the economy and has a bright economic future, it would not for instance be possible to witness the improvements in health and safety at work.

While just a few years ago the thought of a holiday in Bradford would have been thought quite absurd, examples of our industrial age are now being cherished and preserved with the same enthusiasm as the medieval streets of York. There is no lack of interest, as the stream of visitors to Styal, Bradford and Manchester demonstrates. But nostalgia and curiosity alone do little to halt the waste and decay. The choice is either to support those who are working to preserve our heritage, or face the alternative of relying on designers' visions of the past.

Coronation Street therefore is not just the most popular television programme in the country, it is an important piece of social history – a view of a community that has been savagely attacked by the planners of the 1960s and which is, even now, being slowly eroded. Many people who still live in our industrial communities will agree that it is a heritage we must not lose.

10

THE AD-MAN COMETH

Every time we unwrap a chocolate bar, or open a tin of soup, we are throwing away a tiny piece of history. Packaging and advertising gives a unique insight into the way we live and the style of the age. The Industrial Revolution brought manufacturing to the masses, and there are many museums – often in the original mills and factories themselves – where we can still look at industrial processes of the past. Hand in hand with the boom went a consumer revolution of ready packaged goods, which once filled the shops with decorative, brightly-labelled products, now long since discarded or forgotten. Few fragments of history are more ephemeral than the packages thrown out with the millions of tons of household rubbish we dump each year.

But one man avidly collects what we all throw away. Robert Opie has gathered together almost half a million boxes, bottles and jars which were once a familiar sight in our homes and kitchens – all very ordinary things. 'The more ordinary it is, the more I need it for my collection,' he says. There is no better way, he believes, of putting the past in a complete context, than showing the everyday life that the majority of people lived. It is difficult to pin down

when packaging actually started, but in the 1850s brand names began to appear for the the first time, accompanied by coloured, hand-painted labels. In the next twenty years marketing emerged as transport networks covered the country and products became more widely distributed. Alongside it, the manufacturing industry grew to meet the demand. There was a boom in products which helped the housewife get through the cleaning more quickly. Some lasted many years, only to disappear as new labour-saving devices were invented. Starches, for instance, were used prolifically at the turn of the century, but slowly faded from fashion and now, in the age of the aerosol, are almost forgotten.

Every day Robert Opie goes to local supermarkets and antique shops to collect the social history of the future. 'I am trying to build up the marketing story of every product,' he says. 'It is a tall order because one not only has the product, but its history, the

Nostalgia . . . shoes may be as shiny, and custard as creamy, but the advertising will never quite be the same again.

Robert Opie with part of his collection. The remainder fills five floors of a Gloucester warehouse and is still growing.

advertising, the give-aways and everything that helped to put it on the market. My aim is to create a national centre for the study of this very important subject – after all, it is upon manufacturing that the country survives. Its development, and the growth of retail and distributary trades are all very much part of our lives. Indeed it is a modern miracle that we have at our fingers tips 10,000 products which are freely available to us. I would like to uplift the manufacturing industry in the eyes of everyone, so that it takes its rightful place along with the arts and sciences.'

When Robert Opie displayed only a fraction of his collection at the Victoria and Albert Museum, he easily filled a complete gallery. Sadly, the exhibition did not stimulate the potential sponsors he had hoped to help him achieve his dream. So often it seems, finance and history rarely go hand in hand. Until recently the products which stir people's memories remained stored in boxes at his London home. He has since opened a Museum of the Pack Age in Gloucester Docks and hopes it will grow into an important centre for the study of this completely overlooked aspect of our past. Even with a dozen friends saving all their empty containers for him, keeping his collection up to date with the hundreds

The Age of the Cinema; palace-like buildings, plush seating and rich decoration – a place to dream.

of new products on the market each year is a daunting task: 5,000 yoghurt pots alone illustrates the development of this relatively modern packaging.

Among the collection is a highly decorated packet of six tablets of Sunlight Soap, from the 1880s, which illustrates the initial suspicion of mass-produced goods: the label includes a £1,000 challenge to anyone who could find impurities in the product. By the 1920s the paper and printing had become cheaper, and the lettering simple and modern. Thirty years later, with the birth of the supermarket, the entire design of the soap bar becomes aimed solely at catching the eye of browsing shoppers. Ironically, in 1980, Sunlight Soap changed its packaging completely and went back to the old-fashioned designs of sixty years ago, imbuing the product with an established, home-spun image.

Alongside the Horniman's Tea, Andrews Liver Salts, Theobrom Sweets ('The food of the gods'), Shredded Wheat ('Britons make it – it makes Britons'), Thin Arrowroot Biscuits, and Sopal ('It

imparts a delightful freshness to everything washed with it') are the missing links of manufacturing history. Some of these packages, especially the very early ones are proving extremely difficult to acquire for example pre-war boxes of Kellogg's Cornflakes, and the original tins of Heinz Baked Beans. 'Everytime I find something new,' Opie says, 'It gives me a tremendous thrill.'

At least the packets and bottles of our manufacturing past are still around to be seen and appreciated. Other forms of advertising are perhaps no more than distant memories, particularly those of the cinema. The habit of picture-going reached its peak between the wars, when people often attended the cinema twice a week. With the advent of television and home videos, business has declined, but many of us fondly remember the thrill of the lights going down and settling back to enjoy a full evening's entertainment. It really was a big night out, and a relatively cheap one at that. Cinema-goers expected to see two feature films – a main feature and a second feature – and would have complained strongly if they had not. In addition there would usually be the latest newsreel, trailers, a short entertainment film – perhaps a cartoon or comedy sketch – and an abundance of local advertising in the form of cheap filmlets or static slides. Often the entertainment film itself was the commercial – either a cartoon with an advertising pay-off, or a comedy sketch as much as twenty-five minutes long, but always designed as part of the entertainment.

With the growth of the Odeons and other cinema chains throughout our towns and suburbs, films had an enormous influence on the lifestyle of the times. Homes in the 1930s were built and decorated in 'Hollywood' style; hairstyles, clothes, even speech and gestures, were borrowed from the cinema. The sheer indulgence of sinking into luxurious seats, in

Live advertising in the cinema – the refreshing delights of the Lyons Maid girls.

a warm, sumptuous palace of soft lights, attended by Lyons Maid girls, was a chance for everyone to dream. Advertisers saw it as a golden opportunity to sell their products to a captive, comfortable audience.

In the inter-war heyday of films advertisers clearly felt they could not afford to lose the audience's attention, and had to match the quality of the big picture. Commercials were long affairs, dressed up as elaborate entertainment with high production values. Some were made by feature film studios, with complex narratives built into them to the point where the product became almost obscure. A few have survived, thanks to the notion of film archives which sprang up in the early 1930s. 'Our role is to preserve films on a national basis,' explains Clyde Jeavons, Deputy Curator of the National Film Archive established in 1935. 'We regard them not just as art or entertainment, but also as a valuable record of contemporary life and historical evidence. Within that has grown up the idea that even the advertising film has its place. Its value as an artefact should be preserved, simply because it records very cogently our life and times, albeit given its commercial dressing.'

Cinema advertising goes back a surprisingly long way. One of the earliest was for Dewar's whisky, shot in the 1890s by Edison in the United States. Techniques were crude – it was the people, not the camera that moved – and the wonders of the product had to be taken outdoors where the light was better. It is interesting because it is an intentionally humorous film, featuring portraits in a gallery which come to life and share a Scotsman's glass of whisky; finally a silhouette of Queen Victoria is lowered into the fray. A recent survey demonstrated that TV commercials such as those of Joan Collins and Leonard Rossiter, and John Cleese, are highly successful in marketing terms. Humour, it appears, has always been a strong vein in advertising.

The general tone of commercials was aimed at the middle and lower-middle class picture-goer in the knowledge that any working class audiences would be aspiring in that direction anyway. Typical of its kind was a 1920s advertisement for Swan pens, which depicted a failed writer who obviously lived in quite

RIGHT: Clyde Jeavons of the British Film Institute – reliving an evening in the palace of dreams.

One of the earliest cinema commercials, for Vinolia Soap, was shot outside the factory gates for better light. The girls packed the product and the warehouse boy moved constantly to and fro in front of a fixed camera.

comfortable surroundings with a maid, nicely-furnished house, and well-dressed children – though it was not quite clear where his money came from. The writer's career takes a dramatic turn for the better when he uses a Swan fountain pen, and a doey-eyed close-up of his little girl and her baby talk is thrown in to pluck the heart strings.

An Englishman's Home, shot after World War II to advertise Horlicks, makes an attempt to return to solid middle-class English values after the horrors of conflict, by showing a man returning from work and relaxing for the evening in a happy home. The kitten and dog romp on the rug before a welcoming fire, and the Staffordshire china gleams on the mantlepiece. Despite the fact that not too many people today go home and change into something comfortable by taking off their jacket and tie – and putting on another jacket and tie, it was one of the earliest attempts at nostalgia, and has been emulated many times since.

Over the years many themes were used which would today induce apoplexy in the Advertising Standards Authority. Tobacco, for instance, was often sold with the suggestion that it was blessed by the medical profession. Presumably more doctors smoked half a century ago, but a commercial for

Classic Curly Cut pipe tobacco, featuring a GP advising his patient to take up smoking to soothe his nerves, still comes as a surprise. Advertising between the wars fell only under the eye of the film censor whose prime concern was vulgarity and libel.

Two More Cigarettes, which offered the bonus of an extra two per packet for the same price, played on the wise family who smoked them like chimneys and saved enough money for a seaside holiday. They were compared with the silly family who never quite got anything right, and could not afford to go away – a theme still used in television advertising today. The Two More family may not have lived to see forty, but at least they were enjoying a £5 holiday. With the coming of television, a much more influential and wide-ranging medium, tougher restrictions were imposed on advertising.

'It was a heyday for the advertising film,' says Clyde Jeavons. 'Ford, in particular, virtually had a whole film industry of its own. It made numerous short, medium length and quite long magazine-style films, full of matter not necessarily related to the Ford company – just to keep the audience entertained – but every so often there would be a mention of a Ford product. One of their best commercials, *The Rhythm of the Road*, took a more direct approach, but again it was pure entertainment. The audience were invited to sing along, which was a very popular thing to do in the cinema. The production value was very high – the song and orchestra were specially commissioned for the film and they actually set up a King Palmer's Shadow V8 Orchestra, with Gordon Little who was a popular band singer. The song itself was launched at the 1936 Ford Motor Show at the Albert Hall and was quite a big number.

Many of the early advertising films were extremely long, often like documentaries, based on elaborate descriptions of the Cadbury's factory or the Peek Frean biscuit works. Today they are important films, giving an insight into what life was like between the wars. It was only in the 1940s, when film stock became expensive and limited because of the war, that there was a drastic reduction in the length of commercials. Directors used to a more leisurely pace struggled to make their impact in less time and footage.

But if cinema advertisements are interesting because they provide a glimpse of the past, are they also worth saving for artistic reasons? 'Very much

so,' Clyde Jeavons believes. 'In this country, for some reason, there is an extremely strong link between the legitimate film maker and the commercial. Such films are certainly not to be snubbed and thrown away simply because they advertise something. In the 1930s the tradition was powerful, largely through the GPO Film Unit, which accommodated documentary film makers like Humphrey Jennings, Cavalcanti and Len Lye, who did extraordinary experimental work through commercials.

'*Rainbow Dance* for example, which is probably Len Lye's supreme piece of animation film-making, is just advertising the Post Office Savings Bank. Despite that it is a remarkable experimental film in its own right, and often quoted in people's top-ten lists as being a work of genius. George Powell's series of commercials for Horlicks were also inclusive of some quite elaborate puppet animation. He was a fine animator at the start of his career and made a whole series of high-budget Horlicks films in Technicolour to a very high standard.'

Although many of these films were miniature masterpieces the underlying idea was to sell a product. Advertising companies discovered at an early stage that there was a lucrative market in local dealers who loved to see their name up on the silver screen. The first attempts at public advertising were in the theatre and music hall with lantern slides projected onto the safety curtain. The idea continued even in the cinema up to World War I when advertising slides were shown if a reel broke, to keep the audience happy. It was perhaps a condescending attitude to assume that the audience could not sit still if nothing was happening but it all added to the evening's entertainment.

As the cinema moved from travelling fairgrounds to permanent buildings, films were distributed throughout the country and national products were advertised more extensively than local ones. They became so popular that, on the Continent, advertising films were even shown in the streets at night – back-projected with a continuous-loop film on the blinds of shop windows. Britain frowned on the idea because it might have drawn too many crowds and interfered with traffic regulations.

Right from the early days when Queen Victoria was used, albeit in silhouette, to advertise whisky, celebrities and famous faces have been used to endorse products. In 1912 Cadillac made a commercial based entirely around the fact that they had made a miniature car for Prince Olaf of Norway; in the 1920s comedian Walter Ford, who later became a film director himself, featured in commercials. By the 1930s familiar faces were appearing regularly in advertising films – but they were originally the stars of radio, not the cinema. There was a certain novelty in seeing them for the first time and audiences experienced quite a buzz from watching radio stars, such as comic Bobby Comber and bandleader Henry Hall, whose *Guest Night* was listened to by millions. Often they are the only surviving pictures of radio stars in existence, and a valuable record. Henry Hall appeared in a long commercial with his orchestra, playing dance tunes for twenty minutes before the fact that he was selling gas water-heaters became apparent.

The advent of television had surprisingly little influence on cinema commercials. By the 1950s they had already telescoped to something approaching average television length of one or two minutes, and were made on film so that they could be shown both in the cinema and on TV. The first commercial was transmitted as early as 1930, when the Eugene Method of permanent waving was demonstrated on Baird close-circuit TV at the Olympia Hairdressing Fair of Fashion. Even to hoards of preoccupied hairdressers its potential was obvious but it was several years before the plans for commercial television were laid. As it drew inevitably nearer in the early 1950s, strong opposition was encountered, particularly from a vociferous trio of Labour MPs: Christopher Mayhew, Don Chapman and Ness Edwards. The anti-advertising lobby drew the attention of the broadcasting authority, amongst other things, to the shameful transmission in America of the 1953 Coronation ceremony, when the Communion Service was punctuated with advertisements for luxury bedding.

The first British television commercial, for Gibbs SR toothpaste, was allegedly drawn from a hat containing twenty-three other contenders on 22

'Sky Pirates' – a cartoon-length piece of brilliant animation – featured carved wooden figures as members of a rather sluggish air force constantly zapped by the enemy. Finally the problem was diagnosed: night starvation. Liberal helpings of Horlicks enabled the heroes to build a super-airship to put the raiders to flight. Filmed in the 1930s, it was one of the earliest Technicolour cinema commercials.

112

September 1955, and transmitted at 8.12 pm. In technique it was not very different from many of today's commercials thirty years on. The tightly-written copy – 'It's tingling fresh . . . it's fresh as ice . . . it's Gibbs SR toothpaste' – was solemnly intoned by veteran BBC presenter Alex Mackintosh, and the effectiveness of the product illustrated with the aid of a graph. The sixty-second commercial, now in the National Film Archive along with other similar treasures, centred on a tube of toothpaste 'frozen' in a block of Perspex ice, accompanied by a muted string orchestra and the gentle sound of flowing water. Legend has it that the water was provided from the gents lavatory at the advertising studio.

The remaining twenty-three commercials followed throughout that memorable evening, mesmerizing the nation in a dazzling flak of margarine, light bulbs, cheese spread and tinned peas – and netting £25,000 in revenue for Associated-Rediffusion. In the years to follow all the old devices of cinema advertising were trimmed, re-vamped and played to the hilt – from dogs and doey-eyed children to kittens and contented families.

The National Film Archive charts their history with loving care but like the many other bodies who strive to preserve our past, obtaining adequate finance is a continuing headache. 'There is obviously no point in preserving masses of film and television programmes if they cannot be enjoyed and studied in the future,' says Clyde Jeavons. 'It is however a problem of priority and funding – we have a difficult enough time simply preserving neglected films and television programmes.

From about 1895 onwards there has been so much lost over the years that one tends not to be selective. If you find things from that period you try to preserve them. They are often in parlous condition because until 1951 cinema film was made from chemically unstable film stock which began to deteriorate from the day it was manufactured. A lot of this material has to be continuously duplicated onto modern film in order to save it. About two thirds of the early period of the cinema, particularly silent film, has disappeared as a result of natural decomposition, or been destroyed.

In the modern period there is a massive accumulation of film and television and we cannot possibly save it all – we simply haven't the resources or funds. Instead, we have a selection system using consultants, advisers and our own expertise. As new technology appears it is becoming cheaper to duplicate everything onto video tape to preserve it. If we finance this effort properly with public funds, and it is not such a vast sum, then we will be able to continue into the future. . . .'

11

THE AGE OF THE TRAIN

Of all our periods of enterprise and invention, few have progressed at the pace of the age of the train. George Stephenson built the Rocket for the Rainhill Trials, which were the birth of the railway system, when he was forty-eight. By the time he retired to his red-bricked Georgian mansion, high on a hill above Chesterfield, he could look through his study window and watch express trains thundering across the countryside.

As the network spread its fingers across Britain, moving passengers, livestock and raw materials, there were frenzied bursts of building, which reflected the wealth brought by the transport revolution. A maze of railway companies sprang up, some of these went bankrupt, while others merged and lost their identity, leaving behind buildings and bridges which record the life and times of the early railway kings. Today, under the modern mantle of British Rail, many of them serve no useful purpose. So is it better that we forget them and look to the future – or should they be preserved as costly white elephants of a bygone age?

For the thousands of enthusiasts who swarm over the beautiful engines in York's National Rail Museum, the nostalgia of railways is steam. But the real heritage is still around us in the stations, bridges, engine sheds and lines. York, for example, has a magnificent station, one of the largest in the country,

Mechanised muscle – the "Duchess of Hamilton", one of the inter-city expresses of the steam age.

and now a listed building. There is no possible way in which it can be picked up and placed in a museum. The obligation to restore and repair it rests with British Rail, using specially-made bricks and materials designed to look as authentic as possible. It is a costly and laborious maintenance programme and in York's case, immensely worthwhile. Although how do we evaluate the thousands of other railway structures scattered throughout the country in various stages of decay? One answer – and a source of great contention – is to assess their value in relation to the age they represent.

'Some people would argue that nineteenth-century railway buildings are comparable, in their way, with eighteenth-century country houses or medieval cathedrals,' says David Jenkinson, Head of Education at the National Rail Museum. 'Nobody was seriously questioning whether we should repair York Minster after the fire, yet there is a constant problem of what to do about these nineteenth-century structures. It is a difficult problem with no easy answers but one we should be looking at.'

One of the important roots of railway history that has been looked at – and painstakingly restored – is Manchester's Liverpool Road Station, the world's first purpose-built passenger station which linked Manchester with Liverpool thirty miles away. It had separate entrances so that first class passengers would not have to mingle with the travelling hoi-polloi, and separate staircases to take them up to their own waiting rooms. Second class passengers even travelled on separate trains, echoing the value Victorians placed on social structure. What is remarkable about Liverpool Road Station is that it represents a definitive answer to the problem, never previously encountered, of how to construct a railway station.

Just as the railway carriages of the period were modelled on the only available references – stage coaches and farm carts – so the station design was influenced by coaching inns of the 1830s. The station however, was soon found to be in an inconvenient position as the growing number of passengers wanted to be taken into the centre of Manchester. As a result other stations were built with more direct links to the mainlines, closer to the city centre.

It took the efforts of a group of enthusiasts – the Liverpool Road Station Society – to draw the nation's attention to the fact that such a magnificent building was in danger. Eventually Greater Manchester Council grasped the financial nettle and, in time for the 150th anniversary of the Manchester-Liverpool Railway in 1980, decided to make it part of a Museum of Science and Industry. It was bought for £1 from British Rail, who contributed another £100,000 towards it restoration. Today, the unique building looks very much the way it did in 1830, and soon steam engines will once again be drawing noisily out of the low platform, taking excursions to Liverpool.

Liverpool Road only functioned as a passenger station for fourteen years, from 1830 to 1844, but its magnificent warehouses were still being used 130 years later. They were ingeniously constructed so that goods wagons could be lifted straight from the track, turned and swung indoors for loading and unloading. When the warehouses closed in 1975 they became part of a huge burden of railway history that fell to the care of British Rail. The extent of that responsibility lies between the covers of a thick catalogue listing the famous, the not-so-famous and the positively obscure, all needing attention and preservation. They range from a fourteenth-century pulpit in a Shropshire shunting yard, to six sycamores flanking a disused line in North Wales.

'There are some superb buildings in the railway network which have fallen into a pretty bad state,' says Patrick Green, director of Manchester's new Museum of Science and Industry. 'Finding alternative uses – the museum is only one – is probably the only way of ensuring their survival. It is very important, because the railways are such a significant part of our social fabric. To simply lose some of its magnificent buildings would be criminal.'

Patrick Green's sentiments are echoed by David Jenkinson at York: 'As a nation we have a considerable history of preserving our past,' he says. I don't think the railways are different from any other relics of our past experiences.'

One of British Rail's longer and more recurring headaches is caring for the old London, Midland and Scottish, which extended from London to Glasgow. Before it became LMS in the 1920s, and moved its headquarters to London, the centre of the old Midland

The end of an era – the last steam train pulls slowly out of Manchester's Central Station.

Railway was at Derby, a unique station in Victorian times. In the directors' boardroom, the vastness of the Midland empire was represented by a 6 m by 4.5 m (20 ft by 15 ft) canvas map, so large it had to be scrolled up or down to cover the extent of the tracks.

The company was born in the snug of the Sun Inn at Eastwood, a few miles away, where a small group of wealthy local mine owners met each week for lunch. On an August morning in 1832, as the landlord's best wine was being uncorked at half a crown a bottle, conversation turned to the alarming growth of canals. New waterways nearing completion would mean strong competition from other coalfields in the race to sell fuel to the South of England. The Stockton-Darlington Railway, opened seven years earlier, was prospering, and the idea that railways were a useful and successful venture was gaining ground.

The soberly-dressed pit owners agreed to contact an acquaintance, John Elllis, who was a friend of Stephenson, and persuade him to ask 'old George' for advice. When Ellis tracked him down, the tetchy

ABOVE: *Manchester's Liverpool Road Station – the world's first passenger railway station – saved by enthusiasts and the local authority in time for the 150th anniversary celebrations of the Liverpool–Manchester Railway.*

BELOW: *Patrick Green, director of Liverpool Road Station, now part of an enterprising museum project.*

engineer was knee-deep in a Lancashire bog, trying to float a railway line across Chat Moss to Manchester on rafts of bracken. He was clearly in no mood for other problems but after a beef-steak and beer at a local inn (the pub has much to answer for!) he mellowed and agreed to survey a new line for them. The first section was the Leicester and Swannington Railway and over many more meetings at the Sun Inn, it expanded and prospered.

But despite its fortunes, the Midland – unlike other companies – had not extended to London. The lesson of this dawned when the Great Exhibition opened in 1851, and it seemed that half the population of Britain wanted to see the wonders of the world. As everyone poured into the capital, the Midland's bread-and-butter income from holiday routes suffered badly. 'There has been nobody going to Cheltenham, scarcely anyone going to Scarborough, and the little Matlock line has experienced a decline in its receipts this year amounting to twenty per cent,' the chairman gloomily reported. 'All this is actively owing to the Great Exhibition.'

The directors of the Midland Railway were typical of the entrepreneurs who became the driving force behind the Industrial Revolution. They were ruthless, pushy, ambitious, but above all proud of their railway, and determined that it would not suffer again. The board resolved to find a company which terminated its line in London, so it could open negotiations. Despite their domination of the Midlands and the North East, each approach was greeted with a restrained and cautious refusal. Then the Midland, by a stroke of good fortune, remembered that four years earlier, an Act had been passed and never taken up granting consent for a line from Leicester to Hitchin. They applied themselves and, after arranging with another company to run on its lines from Hitchin to London, the great push southward was complete.

Soon the Midland's arteries extended in every direction. After thrusting to the major ports – Bristol, Swansea, Liverpool and Tilbury – enabling raw materials to be brought to the manufacturing cities of the industrial Midlands, they cast their eyes to the growing passenger traffic. Midland Railway policy was to give its fare-paying customers the best possible service. Their first class compartments were luxurious; and they were the first company to give third class passengers upholstered seats, provide

heating in carriages, and build hotels close to the stations. The stations themselves were magnificent – glorious monuments to the company's wealth and success, embellished in house-style and decorated with M.R. insignia, or the Wyvern, the heraldic symbol of the ancient kingdom of Mercia.

Derby Station, used by several companies, all running trains into the town, was for many years the crowning glory of the Midland Railway. A Scottish journalist returning to Edinburgh from London in 1841, described the scene as he stepped from his carriage into the 305 m (1,000 ft) long shed supported on iron pillars: 'Trains coming in and going out, shrill screams of whistles, the hissing of volumes of steam, and the numerous clumps of vehicles belonging to different companies on the complex offset lines – all serve to convey an impressive idea of the magnitude of the concern.'

As the railway grew, and traffic increased, Derby Station was extended piecemeal every few years, until eventually there was no homogeneous building. The main line to London became the most lucrative arm of the company and the station's importance declined. When the old Midland merged into London Midland and Scottish, the network was controlled from London. With the bosses gone and the impressive boardroom empty, the buildings became surplus to requirements and sadly deteriorated. After fifty years of neglect the fate of Derby was sealed – its hotch potch development meant that, despite being in a conservation area, it was not itself listed. The old station, victim of an over-ambitious company a hundred years ago, was recently demolished to make way for a modern complex. The only reminder of its former influence is the frontage, pulled down and rebuilt fifteen miles away at Crich Tramway Museum.

Maintaining redundant station buildings, with echoing empty rooms, is a costly business; the bill for removing dead pigeons from the rafters alone amounted to £2,000. British Rail architect Chris Palmer spent seven years designing a replacement station to meet the needs of changing times.

The complex project was not without its problems: 'Derby was originally designed for horse-drawn vehicles and from what one can gather, it was something of a free for all,' he says. 'As it has grown up, requirements have changed. We now have a pedestrian way into the station, without the need to cross roads. There are bus shelters, areas for taxis to queue, and access for goods vehicles to the parcels office. The new building has to house train crew accommodation, a travel centre, ticket office, buffet, parcels, post office and a bookstall, which all have to go together in a particular way.

Other stations are presenting similar problems for British Rail. Conservation eats up millions, not only in preserving buildings, but tidying the landscape, planting trees and repainting. At Nottingham the council were concerned that the station built in 1857 should be retained as part of the town's railway heritage. It had not seen passengers since 1944, but joint financing between BR and local authorities have made it wind and weatherproof until a future can be found for it. As with Nottingham, British Rail's answer with many old buildings is at least to keep the elements out: 'Dereliction breeds vandalism,' says British Rail Chief Architect Rodney Taylor. 'If you can see that the building is looked after, you stand a better chance of keeping it that way.'

Partnership schemes around the country are often quite small – cleaning up rubbish, or providing hanging baskets to brighten up the platform. British Rail is prepared to discuss schemes with any group, and match whatever they provide pound for pound from its Environment Fund. A Heritage Trust has also been formed specifically to restore historic buildings.

An extensive programme has been carried out at Leicester Station, where Victorian buildings had deteriorated and been demolished. The listed frontage was given a complete face-lift, and modernization undertaken in keeping with the style of the original building. At York, BR faced with patching damaged Victorian brickwork consulted the Brick Research Association to find pits with similar clay and had special mounds made to original patterns. Even small stations have been restored, down to original house colours and travel posters from the early days of steam. Others, like Hebden Bridge, have been maintained by the local staff.

With 2,300 stations to maintain, and 600 listed buildings and structures, the financial burden is heavy. Inevitably some stations, like Derby, have to be rebuilt although Rodney Taylor believes it will be an improvement on the original. 'That is the object of the exercise,' he says. 'To enable people to use it and get onto trains with ease, while adding to the total environment of Derby. I think we can design just as well as our Victorian forefathers, in fact in many ways substantially better.'

But what can many of us do to save and improve, say, our own little local stations? The first step, according to Rodney Taylor, is to use it as often as possible: 'The more custom we have, the more likelihood that the station will remain open. To help personally to improve the environment you could write a nice fat cheque – that would go a long way,' he smiles. 'Or you could write to your MP; you could lobby; you could persuade the Government to give more money to our Heritage Fund; or you could come along and spend a Saturday afternoon weeding the flowerbed, and planting some flowers. Any help is gratefully received, however small. But the real way of saving it is to use the trains.'

The Midland Railway Company, after its triumphant entry into London, wanted to announce its arrival with a building which reflected its stature and prosperity. After much deliberation the result was the overpowering splendour of St Pancras Station. No less than seven London streets and more than 3,000 homes, were demolished to make way for Britain's biggest-ever train shed and next to it, the grandest of station hotels designed by Giles Gilbert Scott.

St Pancras was built on the site of a great battle between Boadicea and the Romans, and ironically conflicts still rage there today. British Rail are left to face the upkeep of a listed building with crumbling cellars and stonework, and rooms too large for its requirements. The root of its problems lies at the northern end of 'Midland' territory, where seventy-two miles of unique and brilliant Victorian engineering – the Settle to Carlisle line – cross the Pennines. It is the only mountain line ever built where trains have run at high speeds of more than seventy mph. But the enormous expense of constructing a route across pastel valleys and forbidding hills stretched the company's finances to the limit. As a consequence corners had to be cut on the magnificent palace of St Pancras. Even as it took shape on the

London skyline, money was tight – the hotel was finished without its top storey, and around the back, where it did not show, inferior stone was used. It remains, however, an exceptional building. The train shed was built with a blue glass roof to give the impression that the sun was always shining, the elaborate precast ironwork, the grandeur of the main staircase and booking hall make it an irreplaceable part of the London scene.

'St Pancras is a fine example of the railway companies at the turn of the century building an hotel to really make an image,' says Rodney Taylor. 'Unfortunately they are not very economic buildings, but nevertheless superb, and must be kept.'

Finance is the perennial problem – restoring the exterior of St Pancras will cost £1.2 million. British Rail ran out of money after completing just a third of the programme. They are now looking for someone to lease the building on a commercial basis to offset costs.

Pressure from the Victorian Society persuaded British Rail to adapt the booking hall, but the staircase, which does not conform to modern fire regulations, is presenting difficulties. To restore St Pancras in a condition suitable for modern office accommodation would mean high maintenance costs on a building which has only fifty-two per cent of usable floor space, compared with eighty per cent in a purpose-built office.

'If someone like the Government stepped in to pay the additional cost, then we could be in business,' Rodney Taylor says. 'It is essential that we keep good examples of our heritage. I think it is wrong to keep everything, but there are some great examples – and St Pancras is one.

'As architects one of our battles is: do you restore St Pancras, or do you keep clean trains running on time and provide a good service? The Heritage Trust and the Environment Fund are ways of balancing the problem. I do not think that there is a real answer – how do you compare keeping a line open with keeping a building that is part of our heritage?' While St Pancras is a protected building, the future of the Settle-Carlisle line hangs in the balance. It was built in the early 1830s because Midland's directors at Derby were unhappy with the lucrative trade other companies were conducting on the main line through the North West. If they could somehow cut across from North Yorkshire to Carlisle, and open a

through-service to Scotland, there would be rich business to cream off. Company engineers virtually drew a straight line on the map across some of the highest and most uninviting hills in Britain, and got down to the job. They threw breathtaking viaducts and bridges across valleys, and gouged out routes through granite mountainsides to open up a path to greater profits. Rail gangs using primitive technology – mainly muscle power – laboured over high, inhospitable terrain, with great loss of life. It was a major achievement of Victorian engineering and architectural skills.

'By any stretch of the imagination the line is something very special indeed,' says Dr John Whiteleg, one of the powerful lobby fighting to keep it open. 'No one who comes to see the Settle-Carlisle line can fail to be impressed by the sheer magnificence of the structures built under such difficult circumstances.' British Rail argue that because of its remoteness, and the number of high-level structures, the line is expensive to maintain. Unlike concrete motorway bridges, masonry viaducts are not easily looked after. They declare, too, that the line is simply unremunerative, and that the small amount of money it brings in falls desperately short of the cost of its upkeep.

John Whiteleg sees the problem in a wider context: 'If you close a railway line, that is not the end of the matter at all,' he says. 'There are many people living in this part of the world, in remote communities for whom it is a lifeline. In their own terms BR are correct in saying that the money they get in fares does not pay the full cost, but if you do not have a railway system you need to maintain roads and bridges. If you do not have good quality public transport, the whole fabric of these areas simply collapses – shops close along with post offices, garages and village schools, and people leave the area.

'We argue that what we are doing to parts of upland Britain for a small amount of financial saving is madness. We are condemning them to a miserable existence. They will become places with just a few second homes, and just a few tourists coming in by car. It is not economic, but we do not expect roads to be economic. They provide a vital service for the community, and the community could not live without them. We put railways into that category.'

Meanwhile the great viaducts of the Settle-Carlisle, built by camps of 2,000 travelling navvies, slowly

deteriorate. For example, the valley crossing at Ribblehead is constructed from limestone, 290 million years old, which has been noticed to crack in bad weather. 'It is a fairly recent phenomenon,' says Alan King, British Rail engineer for the Settle-Carlisle section. 'It was first noticed about 1970, and has got progressively worse. From 1977 to 1983 it had reached the stage where BR considered the only possible solution was to replace the viaduct.

'To replace it with something similar to a simple motorway viaduct would cost around £4.5 million. Repair is a more difficult problem. Over the past five years we have been investigating why this viaduct should fail. The original engineers chose the hardest rock they could find, in fact they diverted a river to get it. But unfortunately the design is just one thickness of stone-facing all the way round, with a rubble-fill inside.

'It is an important line and Victorian engineering at its best. Ribblehead and the other viaducts are ancient monuments, but whether that should be grounds for spending taxpayer's money, to the extent they would have to, is a moot point. As an engineer I admire the line . . . as a manager I cannot see any alternative to closure.'

The problem of the Settle-Carlisle reflects the dilemma of British Rail, and many others charged

LEFT: *Ribblehead Viaduct on the Settle–Carlisle line – cracks in the limestone have left its future in doubt.*

BELOW: *British Rail engineer Alan King on the Settle–Carlisle line: 'As an engineer I admire it . . . as a manager I cannot see any alternative to closure.'*

with the custody of our past. Over the last twenty years we, as a nation, have been increasingly concerned about the march of progress and its disregard for history – and quite rightly so. But the problem is that we have an awful lot of 'heritage', and we cannot save it all, indeed it would not be desirable: to over-collect is to undermine the value of a collection. Having said that we must save something – and therein lies the problem. How do we choose what to save, and more importantly, who is going to pay for it?

There is never any question about our castles and cathedrals. York Minster is being rebuilt after its fire, and I cannot imagine the Tower of London falling into disrepair. But potentially great monuments, like St Pancras, or our urban cemeteries, have unsure futures. And indeed what of the small collections,

which we may view as idiosyncratic, but which will give future generations insight into our lives? The National Film Archive, for instance, struggles to preserve our valuable film heritage while we spend millions on keeping one Renaissance painting in the country.

The pro's and cons can be argued endlessly, and ultimately everyone will say that their personal cause is the most important one – and some will eventually get the funds, and others not. While their arguments go on, perhaps we ought to be thinking about how future generations will judge a society which, for the sake of a relatively small outlay, allows vital parts of its heritage to disappear. To have a sense of the past, it is important to have a sense of the future – but at the moment we seem to have only a blinkered obsession with the present.

Just The Ticket

One of the earliest problems of rail travel was that many people – on both sides of the ticket-office window – could barely read. To make the going easy, some tickets had pictures printed on them to illustrate their destination – a teapot for the Potteries, a thistle for Scotland, a bale of wool for Leeds.

With some companies simply purchasing a ticket was no easy business. Passengers were obliged to give their name, age, address, occupation, reason for travelling and details of their next of kin. Despite the efficiency, fare-dodging was as rife in Victorian times as it is today. Measures introduced to counter it included clamping metal identity bracelets to passengers' wrists, which the guard unfastened at their destination, and locking compartments to ensure that travellers did not jump on or off the train outside the stations. Things changed when Thomas Edmondson invented the ticket machine, which produced tickets by the thousand, each stamped with a serial number and the destination.

Stations Bloom Again

One hundred energetic members of Blakedown Women's Institute, in Hereford and Worcester, rolled up their sleeves, pulled on their wellies and set out to return their local station to its Victorian floral glory. They uprooted weeds, turned over the ground and, with the help of a load of topsoil and gravel, planted shrubs in 100 sq m (1,076 sq ft) of newly-created garden. Each pound of the £112 bill was met with another from British Rail.

The Women's Institute now carries on the good work by keeping weeds down, washing curtains and putting up new hanging baskets, in a scheme which is gaining popularity around the country. British Rail Area Managers are now working closely with Women's Institutes to encourage an interest in local stations, and the scheme may be extended to urban areas through a partnership with Townswomen's Guilds. More than £3.5 million worth of improvements have now been carried out under the pound-for-pound programme.